Murder, Rape, and Torture
in a
Catholic Nunnery

Maria Monk's Awful Disclosures Proven True

Edward Henarie

"I believe that in the end the truth will conquer." John Wycliffe

"For nothing is secret, that shall not be made manifest; neither any thing hid, that shall not be known and come abroad." Luke 8:17.

Copyright © 2015 by Edward Hendrie
All rights reserved.

ISBN: 978-1-943056-00-2

EdwardHendrie@gmail.com

Other books from Great Mountain Publishing:

- Antichrist Conspiracy
- Solving the Mystery of Babylon the Great
- The Anti-Gospel
- 911 - Enemies Foreign and Domestic
- Bloody Zion
- What Shall I Do to Inherit Eternal Life?
- Antichrist: The Beast Revealed
- Rome's Responsibility for the Assassination of Abraham Lincoln

Available at:
www.antichristconspiracy.com
www.mysterybabylonthegreat.net
www.911enemies.com
www.antigospel.com
www.lulu.com
www.amazon.com
http://books.google.com
www.barnesandnoble.com

The author is a contract staff member of the U.S. Department of State and as such is required to give the following disclaimer pursuant to the U.S. Department of State Foreign Affairs Manual, to wit: 3 FAM 4172.1-4. The views expressed in this book are those of the author in his private capacity and do not necessarily represent the views of the U.S. Department of State or any other entity of the U.S. Government.

All Scripture references are to the Authorized (King James) Version of the Holy Bible, unless otherwise indicated. Edward Hendrie rests on the authority of the Holy Bible alone for doctrine. He considers the Holy Bible to be the inspired and inerrant word of God. Edward Hendrie's citation to an authority outside the Holy Bible on a particular issue should not be interpreted to mean that he agrees with all of the doctrines and beliefs of the cited authority.

Table of Contents

Introduction.. 1

1	The Challenge of Maria Monk.	3
2	"She Must be Crazy".	7
3	Infanticide at the Convent..	19
4	Reconstruction of the Nunnery.	22
5	The Underground Tunnel.	30
6	Bible Suppression.	43
7	Dying Declaration..	50
8	Church Sanctioned Murder..	52
9	Proof of Maria's Veracity.	64
10	The Jesuit Scheme of Suborning Perjury.	76
11	Mental Reservation.	83
12	Mass Graves.	87
13	Captive Prisoners.	92
14	Above the Law.	106
15	An Authoritative Exposè of Nunneries..	128

16	Unusual Corroboration..................	150
17	Nun's Island...........................	154
18	Physical Proof........................	155
19	A Nun Corroborates Maria Monk.........	159
20	Masonic Secret Agent..................	164
21	A U.S. Senator Defends Maria Monk......	173
22	The Torture Room.....................	185
23	The Abuse of Nuns Continues............	193
	Endnotes.................................	211

Introduction

There has probably not been a person more maligned by the powerful forces of the Roman Catholic Church than Maria Monk. In 1836 she published the famous book, *Awful Disclosures of the Hotel Dieu Nunnery of Montreal*.[1] In that book, she told of murder, rape, and torture behind the walls of the cloistered nunnery. Because the evidence was verifiably true, the Catholic hierarchy found it necessary to fabricate evidence and suborn perjury in an attempt to destroy the credibility of Maria Monk. The Catholic Church has kept up the character assassination of Maria Monk now for over 175 years. Even today, there can be found on the internet websites devoted to libeling Maria Monk. Catholic Priest J. Bernard Delany, O.P., is typical of the Catholic attacks upon Maria Monk. Delaney alleges:

> The actual facts of the case are simple. Maria Monk was never a nun; she was not even a Catholic, and, although she undoubtedly provided much of the material of the "revelations," she did not herself write the book that has done so much harm and made her name notorious.[2]

I have examined the evidence and set it forth for the readers to decide for themselves whether Maria Monk was an impostor, as claimed by the Roman Catholic Church, or whether she was a brave victim. An objective view of the evidence leads to the ineluctable conclusion that Maria Monk told the truth about what happened behind the walls of the Hotel Dieu Nunnery of Montreal.

The Roman Catholic Church, which is the most powerful religious and political organization in the world, has engaged in an unceasing campaign of vilification against Maria Monk. Their crusade against Maria Monk, however, can only affect the opinion of the uninformed. It cannot change the evidence. The evidence speaks clearly to those who will look at the case objectively. The evidence reveals that the much maligned Maria Monk was a reliable witness who made awful but accurate disclosures about life in a cloistered nunnery.

Edward Hendrie
January 2015

1 The Challenge of Maria Monk

Probably the most famous account of torture and abuse in a cloistered nunnery is the 1836 book by Maria Monk, *Awful Disclosures of the Hotel Dieu Nunnery of Montreal*.[3] The disturbing accounts by Maria Monk brought howls of protest from Catholic authorities and defenders that her book was full of lies. It is notable, however, that the refutation was almost always limited to denunciation and attacks on her character. They dared not seek justice in open court, where the truth of the matter would be determined in public and under strict rules of evidence. The Catholic authorities' objective was to conceal the truth by trying to discredit Maria Monk, not reveal the truth by letting the world view the evidence. The extant evidence substantiated Maria Monk's allegations. Maria revealed the detailed layout of the nunnery, which included an underground passageway leading from the nearby seminary to the nun's convent. The priests regularly traveled through the underground passage to gain entry into the nunnery to engage in all manner of debauchery with the captive nuns. During her lifetime, Maria Monk's character was falsely attacked by the Catholic hierarchy. She steadfastly maintained the truth of her allegations and challenged the Catholic hierarchy to sue her so that the truth of her allegations could be weighed under the rules of evidence in a court of law. The preface to her book states:

> Maria Monk, however, refused to be shaken in her testimony, and steadfastly avowed the truth of what she had written. To those who doubted or disbelieved her statements she made the following challenge.
>
> "Permit me," she said, "to go through the Hotel Dieu Nunnery at Montreal with some impartial ladies and gentlemen, and they may compare my account with the interior parts of the building, into which no other persons but the Roman Bishop and Priests are ever admitted; and if they do not find my description true, then discard me as an impostor. Bring me before a court of justice—there I am willing to meet Latargue, Duireme, Phelan, Bonin and Richards, and their wicked companions, and the Superior and any of the Nuns before a thousand men."[4]

The Catholic authorities did not dare to take Maria Monk up on her offer, as they knew it would have substantiated her charges. They, instead, chose a strategy of obfuscation and suborning perjury. The nunnery was never opened to a tour by her accompanied by objective witnesses, nor were any of the resident nuns ever permitted to be interviewed. Instead, the Catholic church mounted a

MARIA MONK.

campaign of character assassination from a distance. To this day, the Roman Catholic Church is devoted to discrediting Miss Monk. Why do they take such efforts, even today, to discredit Maria Monk? Because the crimes recounted by Miss Monk still go on today inside the cloistered nunneries of the Catholic orders. While Maria Monk's revelations were shocking enough, there were crimes committed inside the Hotel Dieu Nunnery that were so disturbing, Maria Monk could not bring herself to reveal them in her book. Maria solemnly declared that "there are crimes committed in the Hotel Dieu Nunnery too abominable to mention."[5]

The conduct of the priests described by Maria has been confirmed in similar revelations by other escaped nuns in many different countries. The accounts of those escaped nuns corroborate Maria Monk's revelations: Josephine M. Bunkley, *The Testimony of an Escaped Novice from the Sisterhood of St. Joseph* (1855, United States), Sarah J. Richardson, *Life in the Grey Nunnery at Montreal* (1858, Canada), Barbara Ubryk, *The Convent Horror, The Story of of Barbara Ubryk* (1869, Poland), Edith O'Gorman, *Trials and Persecutions of Miss Edith O'Gorman, Otherwise Sister Teresa De Chantal, of St. Joseph's Convent* (1871, United States), and Margaret Shepherd, *My Life in the Convent*, (1892, England).

Rosamond Culbertson revealed how the Catholic priests of Cuba in the early 19th century would persuade the deluded families of Cuba to give them their daughters to enter the convent. The religious and political power of the priests in Cuba was so absolute that the parents dared not refuse the request of the priests. "The young ladies are obliged to enter the convent whether it is their wish or not."[6] The young girls would enter the cloistered convent after solemn ceremony where they parade though the streets, followed by their families and hundreds of priests. Unknown to the families of the young girls, the priestly foxes were herding the innocent hens into the convent for their destruction. The priests talked freely when drunk in the presence of Rosamond Culbertson about how they had planned on ravishing the prettiest of the new nuns who had taken the veil.

2 "She Must be Crazy"

Maria Monk learned the hard way about the power of the Catholic Church, when she traveled to Canada in 1835 and sought to have the civil authorities investigate her allegations of torture, murder, and rape perpetrated within the Hotel Dieu Nunnery. The Canadian authorities were seemingly under the direction of the Roman Church. The authorities took her testimony, but would not take action. What the authorities did do was inform the Catholic hierarchy of the details recounted in Maria Monk's affidavit.[7] The Catholic Church responded by scouring the countryside for witnesses willing to perjure themselves to attack Maria Monk. They also hatched a plan to abduct Maria Monk, which almost succeeded.[8]

Maria Monk's book was widely read and sold over three hundred thousand copies by 1860. Her book revealed the debauchery of the Catholic priests and the cruel rape, torture, murder, and infanticide taking place inside the cloistered nunnery. As popular as Maria Monk's book was in the U.S., it could rarely be found in any bookstores in Quebec, because the bookstores would not risk the inevitable boycott that would ensue by order of the Catholic Church against any bookstore that would carry the book for sale. The Catholic Church was desperate to discredit Maria Monk. They spread scurrilous lies about her. The *Catholic Encyclopedia* is typical of the libelous character assassination leveled against Maria Monk. The following entry in the current edition of the *Catholic Encyclopedia* is found under the title of "Impostors" and lists Maria Monk as a Catholic nun impostor:

> [A]nti-Catholic prejudice is still responsible for a large proportion of modern impostures. Famous among these are the supposed revelations of Maria Monk, who professed to have been a nun for some years in the convent of the Hôtel-Dieu, at Montreal, and who published in 1835 a wild and often self-contradictory story of the murders and immoralities supposed to be committed there by priests and nuns. Though this narrative was fully refuted from the very first by unimpeachable Protestant testimony, which proved that during the period of Maria Monk's alleged residence in the convent she was leading the life of a prostitute in the city, and though this disproof has been in a hundred ways confirmed by later evidence, the "Awful Disclosures of Maria Monk" is a book still sold and circulated by various Protestant societies. Maria Monk died (1849) in

prison, where she had been confined as a common pickpocket (see "The True History of Maria Monk", Catholic Truth Soc. pamphlet, Lond., 1895).[9]

Included with Maria Monk by the *Catholic Encyclopedia* in the list of impostors is Charles Chiniquy. Charles Chiniquy was a former priest, who left the Catholic Church to become the most famous Protestant preacher of his time. For example, his 80th birthday was attended by 2,000 friends and followers, including many prominent citizens and ministers, who gave speeches lauding Chiniquy. His birthday celebration was reported on the front page of the Wednesday, July 31, 1889, edition of the *Chicago Tribune*. Incidently, Chiniquy's 80th birthday was five years after the publication of his book, *50 Years in the Church of Rome*. When Chiniquy died, his obituary appeared on the front page of the Tuesday, January 17, 1899, edition of *The New York Times*, with a eulogy praising his many accomplishments. According to the *Catholic Encyclopedia*, however, Chiniquy was an impostor. The *Catholic Encyclopedia* seeks to deceptively destroy Chiniquy's character and reputation, because they cannot allow him to be believed regarding his revelations about the involvement of the Roman Catholic Church in the assassination of Abraham Lincoln. The evidence proving that the Catholic Church orchestrated the assassination of President Lincoln is detailed in this author's book, *Antichrist: The Beast Revealed*, and in General Thomas Harris' book, *Rome's Responsibility for the Assassination of Abraham Lincoln*.

It is common practice for the Catholic hierarchy to allege that a nun is insane who escapes to reveal to the world the rampant immorality of the Catholic priests and nuns. The entry in *Wikipedia*, which contains libelous traducements of insanity against Maria Monk, is an example of this approach.

There is some evidence that Maria Monk had suffered a brain injury as a child. One possible result of this injury was that Monk was easily manipulated, and was not able to distinguish between fact and fantasy. It has been suggested that Maria Monk was manipulated into playing a role for profit by her publisher or her ghost writers.[10]

What is the source of the alleged head injury story? It was first floated in a false affidavit published in a book by Catholic priests, *Awful Exposure of the Atrocious Plot*, which was published to rebut Maria's book, *Awful Disclosures*. The false affidavit states in pertinent part: "At the age of about seven years, she broke a slate pencil in her head; that since that time her mental faculties were deranged."[11] The author of the affidavit is purported to be Maria Monk's mother. While Maria Monk's mother's name is affixed to the affidavit printed in the book, an original of the affidavit with her mother's signature has never been produced. Why not? Because Maria Monk's mother never signed the affidavit. After the book containing the affidavit was published, Maria Monk's mother revealed that the affidavit was not written by her.[12] She stated that the affidavit was written by someone else; she did not sign the affidavit but was prevailed upon by the Catholic priests not to contest the contents of the affidavit.[13] The book in which the affidavit appeared was so full of provable libel against Maria Monk that it bore no author's name.[14] The book was the deceptive contrivance of the Jesuit priests of Montreal.

The book attacking Maria Monk was so shameful that no one would claim it as his work. The book is the source of the many false averments against Maria Monk that to this day have been used as the basis to assassinate her character and attack her credibility.

Maria Monk's mother's (Isabella Mills) alleged affidavit was witnessed by William Robertson as a justice of the peace. William Robertson was not a detached and objective justice of the peace. He, in fact, prepared an affidavit of his own, wherein he stated that three men brought to him Maria Monk, who he alleges tried to commit suicide by throwing herself into a river. He further alleges that he had her delivered to jail as a vagrant. He claims that he instituted his own personal investigation into Maria Monk and had decided that she was not at the Hotel Dieu nunnery during 1832-33 as she claimed, but lived in St. Ours and St. Denis during that time.[15] Robertson can hardly be viewed as an impartial officer before whom Maria Monk's mother allegedly swore to her affidavit. Robertson seems to have been an asset of the Jesuits, who acted as a justice of the peace on their behalf for the purpose of undermining Maria Monk's credibility. Oddly, Robertson prepared his own affidavit after the alleged affidavit by Maria Monk's mother, yet he never mentioned the mother or any of the facts revealed by her.[16] The affidavit purporting to be the original affidavit of Maria Monk's mother was separately published. The published affidavit of Maria Monk's mother indicated in a typed parenthetical that it was "signed," however, the published affidavit did not in fact bear the signatures of either Robertson or Maria Monk's mother.[17] No affidavit bearing the signature of Maria Monk's mother has ever been produced. That fact supports the assertion by Maria Monk's mother that the affidavit was not written by her, but was the contrivance of Catholic priests, and she refused to sign it when it was presented to her. While Maria Monk's mother refused the sign the affidavit, she shamefully admitted that she agreed with the priests not to contest the averments in the affidavit.

Furthermore, there is an inconsistency between the affidavit purporting to be the affidavit of Mrs. Monk in the book, *Awful Exposure of the Atrocious Plot,* and another publication of what is supposed to be the same affidavit. The affidavit in *Awful Exposure of the Atrocious Plot* does not indicate anywhere that Isabella Mills signed the affidavit. It simply indicates in the jurat that it was sworn before William Robertson. It seems that the publishers were faithfully creating a facsimile of the affidavit that they had on hand. The document that they were working from apparently did not bear a signature of Isabella Mills and so they did not include that information in the book. The separately published alleged affidavit indicates in a typed font in the jurat that it was signed by "ISABELLA MILLS, Widow of the late Wm. Monk."[18] Neither publication produced the actual affidavit bearing the signature of Maria Monk's mother. The reason is that no such signed affidavit exists.

> up these things; they allow their character to defend itself. A few days after, I heard that my daughter was at one Mr. Johnson's, a joiner, at Griffin Town, with Mr. Hoyte; that he passed her for a nun that had escaped from the Hotel Dieu Nunnery. I went there two days successively with Mrs. Tarbert; the first day Mrs. Johnson denied her, and said, that she was gone to New-York with Mr. Hoyte. As I was returning I met Mr. Hoyte on the wharf, and I reproached him for his conduct. I told him tha' my daughter had been denied to me at Johnson's, but that I would have a search warrant to have her when I returned; he had really gone with my unfortunate daughter; and I received from Mr. Johnson, his wife, and a number of persons in their house, the grossest abuse, mixed with texts of the Gospel, Mr. Johnson bringing a Bible for me to swear on. I retired more deeply afflicted than ever, and further sayeth not.
>
> Sworn before me, this 24th of October, 1835.
>
> W. ROBERTSON, J. P.

Bottom of the alleged affidavit of Maria Monk's mother, Isabella Mills, as it appeared in the book, *Awful Exposure of the Atrocious Plot*. Notice, that there is no indication in the jurat that Isabella Mills signed the document. Apparently, the document used as the basis for the published reconstruction was unsigned. Notice also that Robertson's name and the date are written differently from the alleged affidavit below.

> going on; he replied, yes, but they never take up these things; they allow their character to defend itself. A fews day after, I heard that my daughter was at one Mr. Johnson's, a joiner, at Griffintown, with Hr. Hoyte; that he passed her for a nun that had escaped from the Hotel Dieu Nunnery. I went there two days successively with Mrs. Tarbert; the first day, Mrs. Johnson denied her, and said that she was gone to New York with Mr. Hoyte. As I was returning, I met Mr. Hoyte on the wharf and I reproached him for his conduct. I told him that my daughter had been denied me at Johnson's, but that I would have a search-warrant to have her; when I returned, he had really gone with my unfortunate daughter; and I received from Mr Johnson, his wife and a number of persons in their house the grossest abuse, mixed with texts of the Gospel, Mr. Johnson bringing a Bible for me to swear on. I retired n ore deeply afflicted than ever, and further sayeth not.
>
> (Signed,)   ISABELLA MILLS,
> *Widow of the late Wm. Monk.*
>
> " Sworn before me, on this 24th of October, 1835."
>
> (Signed,)   WILLIAM ROBERTSON, M.D., J.P.

Bottom of the published document purporting to be the affidavit of Maria Monk's mother, Isabella Mills. Notice in the jurat, it identifies the document as having been "signed." The publisher would have published the document bearing the actual signature of Isabella Mills, if it existed. No affidavit signed by Isabella Mills has ever been produced, because she refused to sign it.

Once Maria Monk published that her mother stated that she never signed the affidavit attributed to her, the Catholic Church had every interest in publishing the affidavit bearing her mother's signature. The fact that an affidavit bearing her mother's signature has never been published or exhibited to the pubic in over 175 years indicates that an affidavit signed by her mother never existed. Apparently, the facts are just as Maria Monk's mother stated. The affidavit was never signed by Maria Monk's mother, because it was full of lies written by Catholic priests. It was a fraud designed to undermine Maria Monk's credibility and deceive the public. An unsigned affidavit is simply not an affidavit. It is out-and-out deception to characterize such a document as an affidavit.

Maria Monk's mother's refusal to sign the document is strong testimony against the truth of the statements made therein. By falsely purporting the unsigned document as a sworn affidavit, the publishes of the Catholic book, *Awful Exposure of the Atrocious Plot*, committed fraud. Furthermore, to publish the falsehoods in the document as though they were true, the publishers committed actionable libel. The fact that the book was published without any author named, so that no author could be named as a defendant in a libel action, suggests strongly that the fraud and libel were knowing and intentional.

Pastor J.J. Slocum in his 1837 book, *Confirmation of Maria Monk's Disclosures Concerning the Hotel Dieu Nunnery*, explained how an innocuous childhood pencil incident was seized upon by the Catholic priests as their foundation for spinning a false yarn alleging that Maria

Monk was not an escaped nun but was instead a crazy women only pretending to be a former nun.

On page 73 [of the Catholic priest's book attacking Maria Monk], we have the celebrated pencil story. It is as follows: "It appears that Maria, while at school, had her ear perforated by a slate pencil, and that a piece of the pencil has remained in her ear to this day. Her sufferings arising from this cause have been acute, and have led to the supposition that her intellect has been from the time of the accident, seriously and badly affected. It is known to medical jurisconsults, that no question is of more difficult determination than that of alleged insanity. Thus it has happened that the cause of her malady still subsists, and that she still endures its effects." To say the least, this is a curious piece of historic knowledge. There are, however, two statements in it, which are as distant from truth, as the southern from the northern pole. First, the declaration that a piece of a slate pencil remains in her ear to this day, is too ridiculously false to deserve hardly a passing notice.

The origin of the story is this; when Maria Monk was quite a child, she and another little girl were at play, and they put each into the other's ear a piece of slate pencil. Maria says the piece in her ear remained for some time; but she declares, that she cannot positively tell, now, whether it was in her right, or in her left ear. The assertion, therefore, that it remains to this day in her ear, and that she still suffers from it, is destitute of the least semblance of truth. But we are told that the pencil remains, seriously affecting her intellect, and producing, if not absolute insanity, "strange flightiness and unaccountable irregularities." But to talk of an effect without a cause, is an absurdity; and in the present case we see that the alleged cause does not exist. Therefore the alleged effect cannot exist. If Maria Monk is insane, it is unaccountable that none of her friends in New York have ever been able to discover the least indications of it. When her friends call to mind what she has passed through since she left the convent, they wonder that she has not been driven to insanity. Not one female in ten thousand would have endured the ordeal, through which she has been enabled to pass without injury. With an infant in her arms, she commenced the contest. She told her sad tale; but scarce anybody was prepared to believe it. It was too horrible for belief. Hence all about her was suspicion. Her circumstances were suspicious. She was examined, re-examined, and cross-examined by every sort of people. She has been persecuted by Catholics and by Protestants. Malice has directed against her its bitterest arrows of slander. Her feelings have been excited to the highest pitch for days and weeks, for she is naturally very excitable, being constitutionally sensitive. And yet, amidst all her excitements, she has never given any symptoms of insanity while she has been in New York. What confidence, therefore, can be reposed in the multipled charges of insanity which are made against her in the "Awful Exposure?" Sad indeed must be the predicament of truth, if it needs for its support such weapons.

But this charge itself is one of the proofs of her having been a nun. It appears to be the standing order to charge upon every female who makes disclosures, disadvantageous to convents, madness and insanity. Rome set the example. Says Scipio de Ricci, "they say at Rome, to defend the Monks, that the two nuns are mad; but up to the present hour, no one has ever taken them for such." Thus [former nun] Miss Reed was mad or insane, and also [former nun] Miss Harrison, and now [former nun] Maria Monk.[19]

It is the common scheme of the Catholic priests to allege that an escaped nun is crazy and is therefore not to be believed. For example, in 1846 Lady Superior Josepha and a Catholic priest named Calenski conspired to have the priest sexually seduce Barbara Ubryk, who was a newly veiled nun in the Carmelite nunnery in Cracow (a/k/a Krakow), Poland. Barbara resisted the advances of the priest and created a scene by her loud objection. The Lady

Superior Josepha arrived at the scene, and by her conversation with the priest, Barbara discovered that the lady superior was working in concert with the priest. Barbara accused them both to their faces of their apparent lecherous conspiracy.

The priest and lady superior immediately took steps to keep Barbara quiet. Their first step was to spread word throughout the convent that the loud scene was because Barbara Ubryk had gone insane. They then locked her in a eight foot by six foot dungeon. There she remained for 21 years.[20] The other nuns knew that she was in the cell, but were afraid to do anything out of fear of the lady superior and the priest. They probably eased their consciences by convincing themselves of the truth of the allegation that Barbara was insane. Barbara was finally released by the intervention of a kind nun. The nun sneaked down to the cell and upon speaking to Barbara and being convinced that she was not insane got word to the police through an intermediary.[21]

The Catholic Bishop, upon being informed by the police of the allegation of Barbara's captivity, did not believe the allegation. The bishop thus gave the police permission to enter the convent, so that the allegation could be proven false. Upon opening the cell, the officer was shocked and disgusted with what he saw and sent for the bishop, so he could see Barbara's naked, skeletal condition for himself. Upon seeing the condition of Barbara, the bishop withdrew the protection of the Catholic Church from the priest and the lady superior and turned them over to the civil authorities. Calenski ended up committing suicide and the lady superior was criminally prosecuted and convicted.[22]

3 Infanticide at the Convent

Below is Maria Monk's account of the regular practice of infant murder at the nunnery.

It will be recollected, that I was informed immediately after receiving the veil, that infants were occasionally murdered in the Convent. I was one day in the nuns' private sick room, when I had an opportunity, unsought for, of witnessing deeds of such a nature. It was, perhaps, a month after the death of Saint Francis. Two little twin babes, the children of Sainte Catharine, were brought to a priest, who was in the room, for baptism. I was present while the ceremony was performed, with the Superior and several of the old nuns, whose names I never knew, they being called Ma tante, Aunt.

The priests took turns in attending to

confession and catechism in the Convent, usually three months at a time, though sometimes longer periods. The priest then on duty was Father Larkin. He is a good-looking European, and has a brother who is a professor in the college. He baptized, and then put oil upon the heads of the infants, as is the custom after baptism. They were then taken, one after another, by one of the old nuns, in the presence of us all. She pressed her hand upon the mouth and nose of the first, so tight that it could not breathe, and in a few minutes, when the hand was removed, it was dead. She then took the other, and treated it in the same way. No sound was heard, and both the children were corpses. The greatest indifference was shown by all present during this operation; for all, as I well knew, were long accustomed to such scenes. The little bodies were then taken into the cellar, thrown into the pit I have mentioned, and covered with a quantity of lime.

I afterward saw another new-born infant treated in the same manner, in the same place; but the actors in the scene I choose not to name, nor the circumstances, as everything connected with it is of a peculiarly trying and painful nature to my own feelings.

These were the only instances of

infanticide I witnessed; and it seemed to be merely owing to accident that I was then present. So far as I know, there were no pains taken to preserve secrecy on this subject; that is, I saw no attempt made to keep any of the inmates of the Convent in ignorance of the murder of children. On the contrary, others were told, as well as myself, on their first admission as veiled nuns, that all infants born in the place were baptized and killed, without loss of time; and I had been called to witness the murder of the three just mentioned, only because I happened to be in the room at the time.

That others were killed in the same manner during my stay in the nunnery, I am well assured.

How many there were I cannot tell, and having taken no account of those I heard of, I cannot speak with precision; I believe, however, that I learnt through nuns, that at least eighteen or twenty infants were smothered, and secretly buried in the cellar, while I was a nun.[23]

The revelations of Maria Monk were damning to the Catholic Church. The Catholic hierarchy simply could not allow Maria Monk to be believed; so they employed a stratagem of destroying Maria's credibility, while engaging in a scheme to conceal the evidence from the public.

4 Reconstruction of the Nunnery

The Roman Catholic hierarchy has an established pattern of claiming that all former nuns who allege that they have escaped from cloistered nunneries are insane impostors. However, the suspicious conduct of the Catholic hierarchy and their provably false claims in response to the allegations of Maria Monk unintentionally testify to the truth of Maria Monk's allegations.

The Roman Catholic church denied that Maria Monk was ever a nun and that there were no hidden passages, as alleged by her, through which priests could enter the nunnery. It has been known that the nunnery was altered by carpenters and masons to conceal the passages and cells revealed by Maria Monk, once her story became public knowledge. That reconstruction to conceal the hidden features of the nunnery is the best corroboration of the truth of Maria Monk's allegations. In the appendix to her book, it was revealed:

> It is also a fact publicly avowed by certain Montreal Papists themselves, and extensively told in taunt and triumph, that they have been employed as masons and carpenters by the Roman Priests, since Maria Monk's visit to Montreal in August, 1835, expressly to alter various parts of the Hotel Dieu Convent, and to close up some of the subterraneous passages and cells in that nunnery. This circumstance is not pretended even to be disputed or doubted ... But the filling up and the concealment of the old apertures in the nunnery, by the order of the Roman Priests are scarcely less powerful corroborative proof of Maria Monk's delineations, than ocular and palpable demonstration.[24]

Maria Monk was informed that masons and carpenters had been employed to alter the nunnery since she left it and her story became public. Testimony from the workers proves that changes were made to the nunnery, but Maria opined that enough of the nunnery must have remained to substantiate her description. That is why the Catholic hierarchy never took her up on her challenge to allow her along with objective witnesses to tour the nunnery.

What could the Catholic Church do? Their initial refusal to agree to Maria Monk's challenge was suspicious and their explanation that the nature of a cloistered convent did not allow for public scrutiny simply was not believed. They were forced to do something to quell the public clamor that the convent be opened to inspection.

The Catholic hierarchy delayed for over a year while alterations were made to the nunnery and only then brought in observers, who were portrayed falsely as being objective, to view the newly altered nunnery. The people brought in to tour the nunnery could not be openly Roman Catholic; that would make the ruse too obvious. They decided upon William L. Stone, the Presbyterian editor of the *New York Commercial Advertiser* and a few other hand-picked observers. As expected, their hand-picked mouthpiece, Stone, published an article in his newspaper refuting the claims of Maria Monk regarding the layout of the nunnery. That was the whole purpose of Stone's guided tour.

Mr. Stone's publicly stated opinion was not based upon the evidence seen by him, but rather it was a contrived opinion entered into by the collusion of the Jesuits, without regard to the evidence. James P. Miller revealed that Mrs. Shepherd, who, along with her husband, accompanied Mr. Stone in his tour of the Hotel Dieu Nunnery, and she came to the complete opposite opinion from that of Mr. Stone's published opinion. Mrs. Shepherd repeatedly affirmed in private conversations that after the tour she was convinced of the truth of the Awful Disclosures of Maria Monk.

> There was one other circumstance which I state on the authority of a highly respectable lady of Montreal, who travelled in company with Mr. and Mrs. Shepherd of Va., from Montreal to New York, who assured me that *Mrs. Shepherd repeatedly expressed her conviction of the truth of the Awful Disclosures in general after she*

visited the Convent in company with Col. Stone.[25] (italics in original)

How could Mr. Stone and Mrs. Shepherd see the same evidence and come to completely opposite opinions? The surprising answer is that they did not come to opposite conclusions. It turns out that both Mrs. Shepherd and Mr. Stone actually come to the same conclusion from what they saw. They both in fact concluded that Maria Monk told the truth. Both their opinions, however, remained private and were only shared with their intimate friends. If both Mrs. Shepherd and Mr. Stone could not be counted upon to keep their true opinions private, they would never have been allowed to tour the Hotel Dieu Nunnery. Mr. Stone, as the editor of the *New York Commercial Advertiser,* could be further counted upon to publish deceptive Jesuit propaganda. Stone's public opinion was directly contrary to his actual private beliefs. Mr. Stone intentionally lied in his article. As we shall see, Mr. Stone had a strong pecuniary motive to lie.

Stone's deception is manifestly obvious to any informed reader. Stone claimed that he fully explored the entire Hotel Dieu Nunnery in three hours.[26] A knowledgeable architect, who was familiar with Hotel Dieu Nunnery, and in fact lived near it for 21 years, stated that anyone who thinks that they could fully explore the massive building in three hours is either a fool or a knave.[27] Stone was neither a fool nor a knave. Stone was a Freemason, accustomed to deception, who was practicing his craft of dissimulation.

Stone admitted in a booklet he later published detailing his tour of the nunnery that he had not even read

Maria Monk's book. "Of the truly 'Awful Disclosures' of Maria Monk, I had formed no very definite opinion previous to entering the province. Indeed, I had not read the book in any other manner than by occasional and very cursory glance at a few of its pages. Still I had read much *from* and *of* it, and heard much more."[28] (italics in original)

Stone was only a Protestant in name only, as his opinion was that the Catholic Church was a "Christian religion." He admitted that he found it difficult to believe Maria Monk's story. "The tale was most revolting, and it was not a little difficult to bring the mind to believe it possible, that even the most hardened of our species could be guilty, from year to year, of the frightful abominations charged by Miss Monk upon the priests and nuns of Montreal-much less the professed ministers of the Christian religion."[29] How could he make such a judgement without reading her book and assessing the evidence? Obviously, his published opinion was based upon bias and prejudice.

Stone revealed his bias and the undue influence of the Catholic clerics over him by making the incredible assertion that "the whole town and province [of Montreal] disbelieved the narrative of Miss Monk."[30] That was so patently false, it could only have been a piece of propaganda that was inculcated to him by his Jesuit hosts. He was simply passing along the information with no thought to scrutinize its accuracy, because he understood his mission was not to inform but to pass along false propaganda. While the Catholics may have been afraid to say that they agreed with Maria Monk's account, they believed it to be true.

William Stone also claimed that there had been no alterations of the nunnery. "No alteration whatever has been made within the Hotel Dieu Nunnery since the time Maria Monk says she left the place."[31] Stone emphasized that "[t]here have been no alterations either in the building within, or the vaults beneath, or the walls without."[32]

The aforementioned architect, who was knowledgeable about the nunnery, stated that Stone was completely "hoaxed" by the Jesuits and nuns of Montreal into believing that there were no alterations of the nunnery. The architect, who was of the highest reputation and unimpeachable veracity, stated that he, along with 20 others, were working on a building adjacent to the Hotel Dieu Nunnery and could see from the scaffolding over the wall to the rear of the nunnery from Notre Dame street. He and the others were looking over the wall shortly after the publication of Maria Monk's revelations about the nunnery. He stated "there we saw, during last May, June, and July, between 15 and 20 men busily employed within the nunnery's outer walls, carrying in timber, stones, and mortar. The work went on briskly for three months; how much longer I do not profess to say."[33] He stated that the workers were occupied with carrying their materials inside the building and no work could be seen being done in that area on the outside. Indeed, it was general knowledge of the people living in Montreal around the Hotel Dieu Nunnery that the nunnery had undergone massive reconstruction after Maria Monk's allegations came to light.

The architect's name was not revealed, because those investigating the facts feared persecution and business boycott of their sources of information by

Catholics in Montreal. W.C. Brownlee explained that he often withheld the names of witnesses who had first hand knowledge of facts that supported Maria Monk, because "[t]here is a ferocious persecution set on foot in Montreal against all who have the honest courage to utter their free sentiments on the ghostly despots of the priest-ridden city; or who openly avow that they cannot resist the overwhelming evidence of Maria Monk's narrative. ... I cannot be induced to give the name of a friend to the ferocious editors of Montreal and daggers of priestly minions."[34]

Mr. Clary, a Protestant minister, stated that material alterations had been made to the Hotel Dieu Nunnery. In response to Stone's report Mr. Clary stated:

> He [Stone] said nothing about the recent building and repairing of stone walls within the enclosure of the convent, and which everybody who wishes can see, nor the new wall within the building, as mentioned privately by one of the former examiners-nor does he tell us that the well in the cellar was dug this summer, nor whether or not it is in exactly the same place that the cemetery, or hole for smothering nuns and infants is said to have been.[35]

In the course of Stone's attempt to play along with the charade he actually confirmed a statement that Maria Monk made about a door that was hidden from public view, and that she could only have known about if she was a nun in the Hotel Dieu Nunnery. Stone stated: "But here, true enough, we discovered what Maria calls 'a great, gloomy iron door!'"[36] Stone's purpose was to explain that Maria was wrong, because it was not in the same location averred by Maria and it did not conceal the burial pit described by Maria. Instead, Stone stated that behind the door he found a cellar containing a well and pump. The well and pump were constructed and installed that summer after Maria Monk's revelations. It was manifestly clear to any discerning inspection that it was a recently constructed well.[37] Indeed, there was no need for a well, since there had always been two wells in the yard of the nunnery. The hastily built well was clearly unnecessary, except for the purpose of destroying and concealing the lime-pit used for eliminating the remains of murdered nuns and infants as described by Maria Monk.

5 The Underground Tunnel

Priests often came into the Hotel Dieu Nunnery through a secret passage from the nearby seminary to have their way with the nuns. Maria recounts an episode the very night that she took the veil to become a cloistered nun:

> Nothing important occurred until late in the afternoon, when, as I was sitting in the community-room, Father Dufrèsne called me out, saying he wished to speak with me. I feared what was his intention; but I dared not disobey. In a private apartment, he treated me in a brutal manner; and from two other priests I afterward received similar usage that evening. Father Dufrèsne afterward appeared again; and I was compelled to remain in company with him until morning.

> I am assured that the conduct of the priests in our Convent has never been exposed, and is not imagined by the people of the United States. This induces me to say what I do, notwithstanding the strong reasons I have to let it remain unknown. Still, I cannot force myself to speak on such subjects except in the most brief manner.[38]

The nunneries are used as brothels by the priests who pimp out the nuns to wealthy Catholics seeking the thrill of illicit debauchery. Maria Monk and all nuns at the Hotel Dieu Nunnery took a vow "that all officers and citizens admitted into the nunnery in priests' dresses were to be obeyed in all things." Maria saw one man in the nunnery who was not a priest, but he was dressed up like a priest, whom she recognized as someone who lived only blocks from her mother's home. He told Maria that he had paid the priests $500 to gain access to the nunnery through the underground passageway. Clearly, he was there to take advantage of the nuns' vow of obedience. He told Maria that many British officers were admitted to the nunnery in the same manner.[39]

Nuns take a vow of poverty, a vow of chastity, and a vow of obedience. In view of the vow of chastity, one might ask how is it that there is so much fornication in a nunnery that is sanctioned by the Catholic Church? There is a hierarchy in the vows. The solemn vow of obedience takes precedence over the vows of poverty and chastity. Obedience is to be given without question to a command from a superior. The priest is her superior. If a command violates either the vow of poverty or the vow of chastity, the other vows must yield to the vow of obedience. If, therefore, a priest demands sexual obedience from a nun, then she is obligated to suppress her vow of chastity and comply with the demand of the priest.[40] It is a deviant system that implicitly encourages debauchery.

The nuns were forced to submit to the priests' licentiousness through the centuries-old artifice of auricular confession. Maria Monk explains:

> The first time I went to confession after taking the veil, I found abundant evidence that the priests did not treat even that ceremony, which is called a solemn sacrament, with respect enough to lay aside the detestable and shameless character they so often showed on other occasions. The confessor sometimes sat in the room of examination of conscience, and sometimes in the Superior's room, and always alone, except the nun who was confessing. He had a common chair placed in the middle of the floor, and instead of being placed behind a grate, or lattice, as in the chapel, had nothing before or around him. There were no spectators to observe him, and of course any such thing would have been unnecessary.
>
> A number of nuns usually confessed on the same day, but only one could be admitted into the room at the time. They took their places just without the door, on their knees, and went through the preparation prescribed by the rules of confession;

repeating certain prayers, which always occupy a considerable time. When one was ready, she rose from her knees, entered, and closed the door behind her; and no other one even dared touch the latch until she came out.

I shall not tell what was transacted at such times, under the pretense of confessing, and receiving absolution from sin: far more guilt was often incurred than pardoned; and crimes of a deep die were committed, while trifling irregularities, in childish ceremonies, were treated as serious offences. I cannot persuade myself to speak plainly on such a subject, as I must offend the virtuous ear. I can only say, that suspicion cannot do any injustice to the priests, because their sins cannot be exaggerated.[41]

The Catholic officials claimed that there was no tunnel leading to the Hotel Dieu Nunnery through which priests could clandestinely enter the nunnery, as claimed by Maria Monk. William Stone, of course, backed the Catholic claim and stated that "no such passage was ever heard of."[42] Stone emphasized that "no such passage exists."[43] Those statements by Stone were simply not true.

Samuel B. Smith spoke with a witness who saw the underground tunnel that led from the Hotel Dieu Nunnery across St. Joseph Street in the direction of the parish church and the priest's seminary. The witness saw this in the years 1813 or 1814 when workers were employed in digging a ditch for the conveyance of water pipes through the street. She stated that the tunnel was made of stone and about seven feet wide. She stated that it was about four feet beneath the surface of the ground.

Another witness saw a large tunnel exposed while a Catholic cathedral was being built between the Hotel Dieu Nunnery and the seminary. He stated that the tunnel crossed St. Joseph Street at the Hotel Dieu Nunnery and passed on in the direction of the seminary. Smith also talked to a former student at the seminary in Montreal who saw the entrance to the tunnel, which is accessed by way of the cellar under the yard in the rear of the seminary. The witnesses' testimony of having seen the tunnel with their own eyes is strong evidence supporting Monk's credibility. That same testimony is also strong evidence that impeaches the credibility of the Catholic officials, who denied the existence of the tunnel.

On May 5, 1826, almost ten years before Maria Monk's revelations, the Boston Recorder published an account of the subterranean passage that ran from the seminary to the Hotel Dieu Convent. The article was republished in the Canadian newspapers, at which time it created a furor of indignation. The article stated in pertinent part: "In Montreal, a subterraneous pathway leads from the priests' residence to the two nunneries. At Three Rivers where the Jesuits' convent is on the opposite side of the street from the nunnery, a passage under the street formed a communication between the fraternity and the sisterhood."[44]

Mr. E. Sprague, in July 1836, spoke with a gentleman, who was formerly a Catholic, but had become a professed Christian. The man revealed to Sprague the following:

> "[H]e had been employed to labor in the cellars of the Priests' Seminary at Montreal, and while there engaged, he discovered a door in the wall of the cellar, which on opening, he found it connected with a passage under ground. He entered the passage, and passed through it until he came to some stairs, at the head of which was a trap door. From the direction and distance of the passage, he was perfectly certain that it must be a subterraneous communication between the seminary and the Convent. He further informed me that from the testimony of many females, his relatives not excepted, that at confession, the priests were in the habit of asking the most licentious and revolting questions that could be propounded, not only to married ladies, but also to girls of 13 years. Likewise from the habiliments of the Nuns and their appearance at times, he was wholly confirmed in the belief that their course in the nunnery was any thing but virtuous. At the time of his making those disclosures Maria Monk had not written her book. I think testimony of this kind is powerfully corroborative, and that these things exist I fully believe.[45]

On or about 1836, Mr. W. Miller stated that it was common knowledge among those living nearby that there was an underground passage connecting the seminary with the Hotel Dieu Convent. Mr. Miller, himself, saw the underground passage uncovered when some workmen were excavating the area to install water and gas pipes. The workers who uncovered the underground passage went down into it, and a group of pedestrians gathered to observe it. After a short period, some priests from the seminary appeared and prevented any exploration of the tunnel and ordered it to be covered back over.[46]

On or about 1836, one Mr. Janes stated that he spent several years living in Montreal. He stated that in walking from his store to the Post-Office, he generally passed by the large Catholic cathedral under construction near the seminary. He stated that he witnessed the whole progress of the building, from the digging for the foundation to its completion. He estimated that on not less than one hundred occasions he saw the subterranean tunnel leading diagonally from the priests' seminary, across Saint Joseph Street to the Hotel Dieu Nunnery; it was large enough for persons to pass through.[47]

On or about 1836, Protestant minister George Bourne stated that he also saw the opened tunnel leading between the seminary and the convent at the excavation site during the construction of the Catholic cathedral. Mr. Bourne stated that the existence of the underground passage was generally known by the citizens of Montreal, because all who passed by the construction site could see it plainly.

Thomas Hogan was a student at the seminary before he changed his mind about becoming a priest. On October 6, 1836, he signed an affidavit under oath that revealed that there was an underground passage running from the seminary to the Hotel Dieu Convent, just as described by Maria Monk.

> Thomas Hogan, of the city of New York, being duly affirmed, doth say, —that in the year 1824, he was a resident of the city of Montreal, Lower Canada ; and that at that period, the existence of a subterranean passage between the seminary in Notre Dame street, and the Hotel Dieu Convent, was a matter of the most public notoriety; and that he himself has been in that passage, having entered it from the door in the seminary; and the said Hogan doth further depose, that to his own personal knowledge, the Roman priests were constantly in the practice of visiting the nuns for the purposes of licentious intercourse, by that secret passage. Affirmed the twenty-sixth day of October, 1836—before me. WM. H. BOGARDUS, Commissioner of Deeds.

When Mr. Stone contradicted Mr. Hogan's affidavit, Mr. Hogan responded by vehemently reaffirming the truth of his previous affidavit and, in effect called Mr. Stone a liar who was engaging with the Jesuits in a deliberate fraud upon the public.

> William L. Stone contradicts my affidavit of October 26. He says that my affidavit "proves too much." I know that fact, *it proves too much for the credit of his*

character and conduct. However, what I have said is true! and no Roman priest in Montreal or New York, will venture to dispute its truth before my face, or under his own name will put me to the proof. Nor will Mr. Hall, the partner of Mr. Stone, venture to deny my statements, or call upon me to prove them according to our discipline. He is a Methodist as well as myself; and he knows how to make me speak truth, or to convict me of falsehood: and I hereby call upon him if he pleases to bring me to that Christian test.

As to the way by which I became acquainted with the abominable practices of Mr. Stone's dear friends and "agreeable travelling companions," the Canadian Jesuits, that is of no importance. I have solemnly affirmed several facts, which no upright and intelligent man will contradict; for not one man in Canada believes Mr. Stone's fictions; and many Papists as well as Protestants, both in Canada and New-York, laugh at his imprudence in attempting to impose upon the American churches—while all the Roman priests, both in the United States and in that Providence, so delight in his extravagant falsehoods, that it is proposed by one of the popish papers of New York, to purchase "a handsome piece of plate to present to Colonel Stone, as a small token of Catholic gratitude for Protestant advocacy."

To my utter surprise; Mr. Stone continues boldly to repeat three things which are so notoriously untrue, that it seems scarcely possible to believe that his words are real.

1. Mr. Stone says, that "no alterations have been made in the Hotel Dieu Convent." Upon that subject he is totally wrong; for I have abundant testimony to prove that the inside of the house has been altered. As 1 know something; about building, which Mr. Stone, notwithstanding his "iron pointed cane," is not acquainted with; if he will get permission for me and three companions to go into the house, I will show him where It has been altered. But my old acquaintances, the Roman Priests of Montreal, never will let me and my associates enter the apartments of the Nunnery.

2. Mr. Stone still denies the existence of the subterranean passage; he may as well deny the existence of Wall-street in New York. He says, that "the Cathedral is in the way;" but the contrary is the fact, for the passage runs close by the Cathedral, as multitudes of people in Montreal attest, not only Protestants but Papists. That the passage did exist in 1824, and is still used for the secrecy and facility of intercourse between the priests and nuns, is well known to all Montreal. That passage to my

own personal knowledge, is also the way by which the priests led the nuns from the Convent, carried them to the Seminary, put on them priest s clothes, and in that disguise as priests, took the nuns to the priest's farm, and to Nun's Island. If Mr. Stone denies it, then it only shows that he is ignorant or a deceiver.

3. Mr. Stone also repeats his amazing contradictions about the size of the Nunnery. I am convinced that the mass-house alone, with the nuns' chapel adjoining, covers as much space as the New York Brideweli.— There cannot be two more plain and astonishing falsehoods than Mr. Stone asserts about the subterranean passage and the size of the convent. There is not one word of truth in his statement!

I therefore most solemnly affirm the truth of my former testimony; and from my own personal knowledge again declare, that the subterranean passage between the Seminary and Nunnery was in existence in the year 1824; and that it was well known to many Papists in Montreal, to be constantly used for the most criminal purposes— and that there is no more truth in Mr. Stone's statement respecting the size of the Hotel Dieu Convent, than if he were to maintain, that a stout dray horse is no larger than a young suckling calf— and I am convinced that Mr. Hall knows my statement to be "the truth, and nothing but the truth."

THOMAS HOGAN.[48]

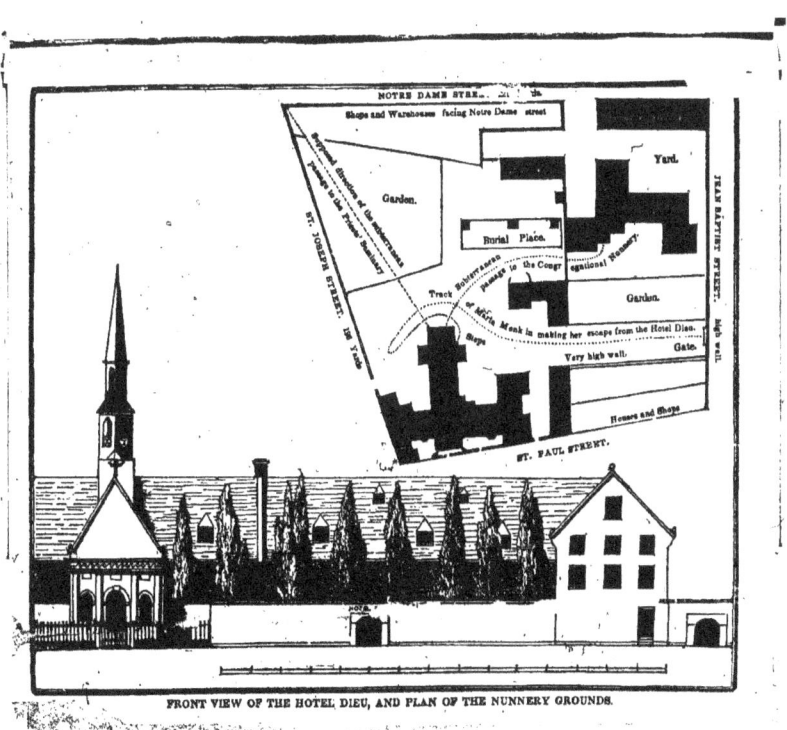

FRONT VIEW OF THE HOTEL DIEU, AND PLAN OF THE NUNNERY GROUNDS.

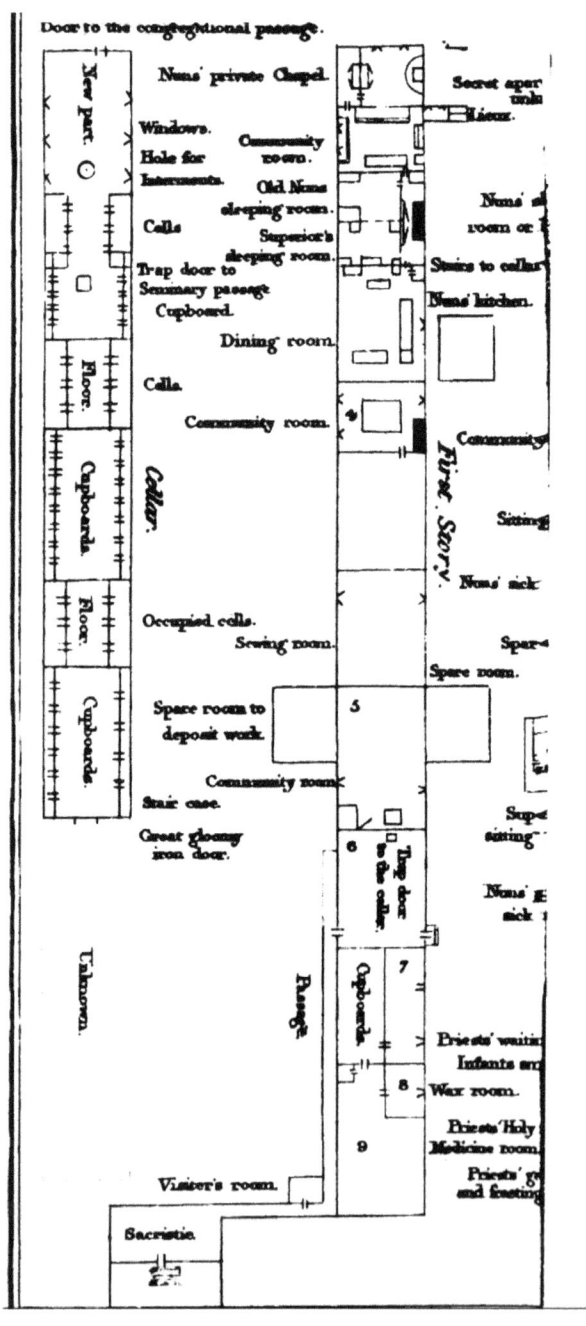

6 Bible Suppression

William Stone's purpose of defending the Jesuit priests was clearly manifested in one particular lie he passed along from one of his hosts, Bishop M'Donald. Stone stated: "Bishop M'Donald is a Scotch gentleman of the old school; affable, intelligent, and for a Catholic, not intolerant. He allows his people to read the Bible, and gives away all that he can obtain for that object."[49] That patent falsehood conveyed by Stone was said to refute Maria Monk's claim that the priests taught the children in school not to read the bible. The Catholic Church is so famously the enemy of the word of God, the falsity of the claim made to Stone by the bishop of fidelity to the bible could only be believed by the most naive of persons. There is little doubt that Stone knew it was not true when he heard it. Stone was a willing participant in a charade.

A protestant group who reviewed the claims of Stone regarding bible distribution by the Catholic hierarchy had this to say:

> We deliberately pronounce the assertion to be a scandalous and notorious specimen of the Popish "all deceivableness of unrighteousness." Mr. Stone knows it is a mischievous falsehood, which is promulgated by him to deceive the Christian public and paralyze the efforts of those philanthropists who are anxious to diffuse the holy scriptures among the Canadien population who are destitute of the bible.[50]

Maria Monk gives the following account of her Catholic instruction when she was a student at the congregational nunnery, regarding the reading of the Holy Bible:

> Among the instructions given us by the priests, some of the most pointed were those directed against the Protestant Bible. They often enlarged upon the evil tendency of that book, and told us that but for it many a soul now condemned to hell, and suffering eternal punishment, might have been in happiness. They could not say any thing in its favour: for that would be speaking against religion and against God. They warned us against it, and represented it as a thing very dangerous to our souls. In confirmation of this, they would repeat some of the answers taught us at catechism, a few of which I will here give. We had little catechisms ("Le Petit Catechism") put

into our hands to study; but the priests soon began to teach us a new set of answers, which were not to be found in our books, and from some of which I received new ideas, and got, as I thought, important light on religious subjects, which confirmed me more and more in my belief in the Roman Catholic doctrines. These questions and answers I can still recall with tolerable accuracy, and some of them I will add here. I never have read them, as we were taught them only by word of mouth. ...

_Q_. "Why did not God make all the commandments?"

_A_. "Because man is not strong enough to keep them."

And another.

_Q_. "Why are men not to read the New Testament?"

_A_. "Because the mind of man is too limited and weak to understand what God has written."

These questions and answers are not to be found in the common catechisms in use in Montreal and other places where I have been, but all the children in the Congregational Nunnery were taught them, and many more not found in these books.[51]

The truth of Maria's account regarding the Catholic doctrinal biblio-animus is found in the official encyclicals issued by the mythically infallible popes, both before and after Maria Monk was catechized. On May 5, 1824, Pope Leo XII issued his encyclical *Ubi Primum* which exhorted the bishops to remind their flocks not to read the Bible. On May 24, 1829, Pope Pius VIII issued the encyclical *Traditi Humilitati,* which exhorted Catholics to check the spread of Bibles translated into the vernacular, because those Bibles endangered the "sacred" teachings of the Catholic Church. On May 8, 1844, Pope Gregory XVI issued his encyclical *Inter Praecipuas* in which he described Bible societies as plotting against the Catholic faith by providing Bibles to the common people, whom he referred to as "infidels."

The catechism to which Maria Monk referred was consistent with the official catholic doctrine of the Vatican. In view of those papal encyclicals, it seems a little ridiculous for the priests to pretend that the Catholic Church is trying to spread the word of God; particularly when everyone who has read the bible knows that at the turn of every page in the bible one finds an impeachment of Catholic dogma, and it is therefore clearly not in the Vatican's interest to see the word of God spread. In fact, to spread the word of God, would be considered rebellion against the official edicts of the pope, who is the monarchial head of the church. Revealingly, when Stone described the books in the nuns' quarters at the Hotel Dieu Nunnery, he did not mention once the presence of a bible, which one would think would be prominently displayed, if it was commonly used.

During a debate with a Protestant minister in the

19th century, a Catholic priest stated that "certain Protestants repeat that the [Catholic] Church forbids the reading of the Holy Bible by the people. That is a cowardly lie, and it is only the ignorant or the silly amongst Protestants who at present believe this ancient fabrication of heresy."[52] That priest called the pastors who made such allegations "unscrupulous" and their believing flocks "dupes." He gave the example of the availability of the Catholic versions of the bible in bookstores throughout Canada, the United States, and Europe as proof that the allegation that the Catholic Church suppresses the bible is not true.

The Catholic priest quoted in the debate above was Charles Chiniquy. He later left the Catholic priesthood and became one of the most famous Protestant preachers of the 19th century. Charles Chiniquy admitted that as a Catholic priest he had engaged in misleading statements like those in the above quoted debate. After Chiniquy left the Catholic Church, he explained that while Catholics are allowed to have bibles in Protestant countries, that is not the wish of the Catholic Church. The Catholic Church only permits such sales, because without political hegemony over a country, the Catholic Church must allow Catholics to possess Catholic bibles. However, Catholics are admonished by their priests never to interpret the scriptures according to their own understanding. A Catholic must always look to the "infallible" Church of Rome in all spiritual matters.

One major distinction between a Catholic mass and a Protestant service is that almost every Protestant can be seen carrying his bible to the service, whereas almost all Catholics will be walking into the Catholic Church building with empty hands. If a Catholic is carrying anything, it is usually a book called a Catholic missal. The missal looks like a bible, but it only contains the instructions, chants, and rituals of the Catholic Mass. Catholics will often say that the fact that they have in their home a Catholic Douay bible is evidence that it is a slanderous lie that the Catholic Church suppresses the bible. Chiniquy responds to that claim, and in doing so impeaches the position he took as a Roman Catholic priest; his response reveals the subtlety of his prior Catholic deception:

> To whom do they owe the privilege [of possessing a bible]? Is it the Church of Rome? Not at all. It is their Protestant friends, to the Protestant countries in which they live. Were they at Rome, they would be put in jail for the same thing allowed to them here. Then, if the Church of Rome permits the reading of the Scriptures, it is not because she likes that, but because she cannot help herself. The light is so near the eyes of the Roman Catholics of this country that it can't be entirely put out from them.[53]

How does Rome treat bible possession when it gains political hegemony? One example, out of many thousands, was the burning at the stake of William Tyndale in 1536, for the crime of translating the Holy Scriptures into English and making them available to the people.[54]

In 1832, Rebecca Reed, as a candidate to be a nun, spent six months in the Ursuline Convent in Charlestown, Massachusetts, before escaping and exposing the cruelty and oppression of the nunnery. Miss Reed never saw a bible the entire time she was in the convent. All requests made by her to obtain a bible were ignored. She recalls the bishop stating that the laity were not qualified to expound on the scriptures and that only the successors of the apostles were authorized to interpret them.[55]

Bible suppression is the rule in Catholic nunneries. During 1854, Josephine Bunkley spent ten months confined in the Convent of St. Joseph in Emettsburg, Maryland, as a nun in the order of the "Sisters of Charity." Miss Bunkley stated: "During the whole period of my connection with the Church of Rome, no such [bible] instruction or counsel was given me by my spiritual director; and while a resident at St. Joseph's, *I never saw a Bible*, and I had frequent access to the library."[56] (italics in original)

7 Dying Declaration

In order to understand why Maria Monk should be believed, one should understand how her revelations came to light. Maria Monk never spoke of her ordeal at the nunnery until she was taken ill at an almshouse and was not expected to live. Believing that she was near death, she summoned for the chaplain, Mr. Tappan, and told him that she had something to communicate to him, and that she could not die in peace without disclosing it. She then disclosed the horrors of her experience as a cloistered nun at the Hotel Dieu Nunnery.[57] She witnessed priestly fornication with the nuns, the killing of the resulting newborn infants, torture, and she was forced to assist in the murder of a fellow nun. She wanted to unburden her conscience about these abominations before she died. At the time she was still under the superstitious beliefs of the Roman Catholic religion and thought it was necessary to make an auricular confession in order to have her sins forgiven before death. She had no intention on making the matter public, as she was still under the superstitious Catholic belief that her auricular confession would be kept inviolably secret.

    Maria Monk survived her illness, and upon recovery she was convinced to write her book documenting her ordeal. It is beyond belief that a person would tell a lie when she believed that she was at death's door, especially when nothing could be gained by it. Such a dying declaration is inherently trustworthy. It is an accepted maxim that no person wants to die with a lie on her lips. Poet Edward Young (1683-1765) succinctly stated the truth:"A death-bed is a detector of the heart."

8 Church Sanctioned Murder

After taking the veil in the nunnery, the nuns were renamed after Catholic saints. For example, Maria Monk was renamed Saint Eustace.[58] That name was given to her upon taking her vows and entering the cloistered order of nuns. Upon taking the veil as a cloistered nun, Maria was directed to take part in a ceremony where she laid in a coffin covered by a suffocating black cloth. The coffin had her new name engraved upon it: SAINT EUSTACE. The coffin was to be stored in a building on the convent grounds and used to bury her when she died.[59] Thus it was made clear to her that she could never leave the nunnery; her only release was through death. The founder of the Church of Satan, Anton LaVey, stated that coffin ceremonies are characteristic of satanic societies (e.g., Skull & Bones, a/k/a Brotherhood of Death). Below is Maria Monk's account of the Murder of a fellow nun known only to her as "Saint Francis:"

I must now come to one deed, in which I

had some part, and which I look back upon with greater horror and pain, than any occurrences in the Convent, in which I was not the principal sufferer. It is not necessary for me to attempt to excuse myself in this or any other case. Those who have any disposition to judge fairly, will exercise their own judgment in making allowances for me, under the fear and force, the commands and examples, around me. I, therefore, shall confine myself, as usual, to the simple narrative of facts. The time was about five months after I took the veil; the weather was cool, perhaps in September or October. One day, the Superior sent for me and several other nuns, to receive her commands at a particular room. We found the Bishop and some priests with her; and speaking in an unusual tone of fierceness and authority, she said, "Go to the room for the Examination of Conscience, and drag Saint Francis up-stairs." Nothing more was necessary than this unusual command, with the tone and manner which, accompanied it, to excite in me most gloomy anticipation. It did not strike me as strange, that St. Francis should be in the room to which the Superior directed us. It was an apartment to which we were often sent to prepare for the communion, and to which we voluntarily went, whenever we felt the compunctions which our ignorance of duty, and the misinstructions we received, inclined us to seek relief from self-reproach. Indeed, I had seen her there a little before. What terrified me was, first, the Superior's angry manner, second, the expression she used, being a French term, whose peculiar use I had learnt in the Convent, and whose meaning is rather softened when translated into "drag"; third, the place to which we were directed to take the interesting young nun, and the persons assembled there as I supposed to condemn her. My fears were such, concerning the fate that awaited her, and my horror at the idea that she was in some way to be sacrificed, that I would have given anything to be allowed to stay where I was. But I feared the consequence of disobeying the Superior, and proceeded with the rest towards the room for the examination of conscience.

The room to which we were to proceed from that, was in the second story, and the place of many a scene of a shameful nature. It is sufficient for me to say, after what I have said in other parts of this book, that things had there occurred which made me regard the place with the greatest disgust. Saint Francis had appeared melancholy for some time. I well knew that she had cause, for she had been repeatedly subject to trials which I need not name—our common lot. When we reached the room where we had been bidden to seek her, I entered the door, my companions standing behind me, as the place was so small as hardly to hold five persons at a time. The young nun was standing alone near the middle of the room; she was probably about twenty, with light hair, blue eyes, and a very fair complexion. I spoke to her in a compassionate voice, but at the same time with such a decided manner, that she comprehended my full meaning.

"Saint Francis, we are sent for you."

Several others spoke kindly to her, but two addressed her very harshly. The poor creature turned round with a look of meekness, and without expressing any unwillingness or fear, without even speaking a word, resigned herself to our hands. The tears came into my eyes. I had not a moment's doubt that she considered her fate as sealed, and was already beyond the fear of death. She was conducted, or rather hurried to the staircase, which was near by, and then seized by her limbs and clothes, and in fact almost dragged up-stairs, in the sense the Superior had intended. I laid my own hands upon her—I took hold of her too, more gentle indeed than some of the rest; yet I encouraged and assisted them in carrying her. I could not avoid it. My refusal would not have saved her, nor prevented her being carried up; it would only have exposed me to some severe punishment, as I believed some of my companions, would have seized the first opportunity to complain of me.

All the way up the staircase, Saint Francis spoke not a word, nor made the slightest resistance. When we entered with her the room to which she was ordered, my heart sank within me. The Bishop, the Lady Superior, and five priests, namely, Bonin, Richards, Savage, and two others, I now ascertained, were assembled for her trial, on some charge of great importance.

When we had brought our prisoner before them, Father Richards began to question her, and she made ready but calm replies. I cannot pretend to give a connected account of what ensued: my feelings were wrought up to such a pitch, that I knew not what I did, nor what to do. I was under a terrible apprehension that, if I betrayed my feelings which almost overcame me, I should fall under the displeasure of the cold-blooded persecutors of my poor innocent sister; and this fear on the one hand, with the distress I felt for her on the other, rendered me almost frantic. As soon as I entered the room, I had stepped into a corner, on the left of the entrance, where I might partially support myself, by leaning against the wall, between the door and window. This support was all that prevented me from falling to the floor, for the confusion of my thoughts was so great, that only a few of the words I heard spoken on either side made any lasting impression upon me. I felt as if struck with some insupportable blow; and death would not have been more frightful to me. I am inclined to the belief, that Father Richards wished to shield the poor prisoner from the severity of her fate, by drawing from her expressions that might bear a favorable construction. He asked her, among other things, if she was not sorry for what she had been overheard to say, (for she had been betrayed by one of the nuns,) and if she would not prefer confinement in the cells, to the punishment which was threatened her. But the Bishop soon interrupted him, and it was easy to perceive, that he considered her fate as sealed, and was determined she should not escape. In reply to some of the questions put to her, she was silent; to others I heard her voice reply that she did not repent of words she had uttered, though they had been reported by some of the nuns who had heard them; that she still wished to escape from the Convent; and that she had firmly resolved to resist every attempt to compel her to the commission of crimes which she detested. She added, that she would rather die than cause the murder of harmless babes.

"That is enough, finish her!" said the Bishop.

Two nuns instantly fell upon the young woman, and in obedience to directions, given by the Superior, prepared to execute her sentence.

She still maintained all the calmness and submission of a lamb. Some of those who took part in this transaction, I believe, were as unwilling as myself; but of others I can safely say, that I believe they delighted in it. Their conduct certainly exhibited a most blood-thirsty spirit. But, above all others present, and above all human fiends I ever saw, I think Sainte Hypolite was the most diabolical. She engaged in the horrid task with all alacrity, and assumed from choice the most revolting parts to be performed. She seized a gag, forced it into the mouth of the poor nun, and when it was fixed between her extended jaws, so as to keep them open at their greatest possible distance, took hold of the straps fastened at each end of the stick, crossed them behind the helpless head of the victim, and drew them tight through the loop prepared, as a fastening.

The bed which had always stood in one part of the room, still remained there; though the screen, which had usually been placed before it, and was made of thick muslin, with only a crevice through which a person behind might look out, had been folded up on its hinges in the form of a W, and placed in a corner. On the bed the prisoner was laid with her face upward, and then bound with cords, so that she could not move. In an instant another bed was thrown upon her. One of the priests, named Bonin, sprung like a fury first upon it, and stamped upon it, with all his force. He was speedily followed by the nuns, until there were as many upon the bed as could find room, and all did what they could, not only to smother, but to bruise her. Some stood up and jumped upon the poor girl with their feet, some with their knees, and others in different ways seemed to seek how they might best beat the breath out of her body, and mangle it, without coming in direct contact with it, or seeing the effects of their violence. During this time, my feelings were almost too strong to be endured. I felt stupefied, and was scarcely conscious of what I did. Still, fear for myself remained in a sufficient degree to induce me to some exertion, and I attempted to talk to those who stood next, partly that I might have an excuse for turning away from the dreadful scene.

After the lapse of fifteen or twenty minutes, and when it was presumed that the sufferer had been smothered, and crushed to death, Father Bonin and the nuns ceased to trample upon her, and stepped from the bed. All was motionless and silent beneath it.

They then began to laugh at such inhuman thoughts as occurred to some of them, rallying each other in the most unfeeling manner, and ridiculing me for the feelings which I in vain endeavored to conceal. They alluded to the resignation of our murdered companion, and one of them tauntingly said, "She would have made a good Catholic martyr." After spending some moments in such conversation, one of them asked if the corpse should be removed. The Superior said it had better remain a little while. After waiting a short time longer, the feather-bed was taken off, the cords unloosed, and the body taken by the nuns and dragged down stairs. I was informed that it was taken into the cellar, and thrown unceremoniously into the hole which I have already described, covered with a great quantity of lime, and afterwards sprinkled with a liquid, of the properties and name of which I am ignorant. This liquid I have seen poured into the hole from large bottles, after the necks were broken off, and have heard that it is used in France to prevent the effluvia rising from cemeteries.

I did not soon recover from the shock caused by this scene; indeed it still recurs to me, with most gloomy impressions. The next day there was a melancholy aspect over everything, and recreation time passed in the dullest manner; scarcely anything was said above a whisper.

I never heard much said afterward about Saint Francis.[60]

The account given by Maria Monk of the murder of Saint Francis is inherently credible, because within the account she tells of the part she played as an accomplice in the murder of the doomed nun. Such an admission against her penal interests must have been difficult. An admission of guilt is always admissible against the declarant in a criminal prosecution of the declarant. Courts view such out of court statements against penal interests as so inherently trustworthy that they are also admissible against accomplices in the crime, if the declarant is unavailable to personally appear as a witness at the trial.

Ordinarily, an out of court statement of an accomplice to a crime sought to be introduced to prove the truth of the matter asserted would be considered hearsay and thus inadmissible as evidence in court, if it is sought to be used against the other accessories to the crime. The declarant would have to personally appear in court and repeat the account for it to be admissible as evidence against accomplices. However, if the out of court statement is against the unavailable declarant's penal interest, that statement is considered so inherently trustworthy that it is admissible against accomplices to the crime. Someone else who heard the statement could testify in court to what he heard the unavailable declarant say. Such was the rule in 1836, when Maria Monk made the statement, and it remains the rule to this day. Virtually every state in the United States allows such an out of court statement to be introduced to prove the truth of the matter asserted. Such statements are today also admissible in federal court.

The U.S. Federal Rules of Evidence has codified this exception to the hearsay rule (which is typical of the rule in most states) that provides that the rule against hearsay will not prevent a statement from being introduced in court when the declarant is unavailable if it is "a statement that a reasonable person in the declarant's position would have made only if the person believed it to be true because, when made, it was so contrary to the declarant's proprietary or pecuniary interest or had so great a tendency to invalidate the declarant's claim against someone else or to expose the declarant to civil or criminal liability; and is supported by corroborating circumstances that clearly indicate its trustworthiness, if it is offered in a criminal case as one that tends to expose the declarant to criminal liability."[61]

One might argue that Maria Monk could not herself be guilty of homicide, because she took part in the crime under duress. There is a defense of duress, if a person is threatened or coerced into committing a crime. The defense of duress is recognized in the law for a person who is put in reasonable fear of imminent death or serious physical injury and there was no reasonable opportunity to escape the harm without committing the crime. However, duress is never a defense to a homicide. The law simply does not allow a person to kill another out of fear that she may be killed herself. The duress may mitigate the degree of homicide, but it is not a defense.

The point of this discussion is not to contend that the out of court statements of Maria Monk regarding the murder of Saint Francis would be admissible in court during a prosecution of the other accomplices in Quebec, Canada. Rather, the point is that her statements regarding the event were so clearly against her penal interests as to render them inherently trustworthy under the principles of common law, which have been established over hundreds of years, by hundreds of jurists, in hundreds of cases. Maria Monk's statement implicating herself as an accomplice in a murder has the indicia of trustworthiness that stamps her account of life in the nunnery with the seal of authenticity. Maria Monk's only objective in her book was to tell the truth, the whole truth, and nothing but the truth, about the netherworld of murder, rape, and torture at the Hotel Dieu Nunnery.

9 Proof of Maria's Veracity

The verification of the truth of Maria Monk's book came in many forms, one of which was explained in an appendix to a second edition of Maria Monk's book:

> We will however state one very recent occurrence, because it seems to us, that it alone is almost decisive of the controversy. A counselor of Quebec--his name is omitted merely from delicacy and prudential considerations--has been in New York since the publication of the "Awful Disclosures" His mind was so much influenced by the perusal of that volume, that he sought out the Authoress, and most closely searched into the credibility of her statements. Before the termination of the interview, that gentleman became so convinced of the truth of the picture which Maria Monk drew of the interior of the

Canadian Nunneries, that he expressed himself to the following effect:—"My daughter, about 15 years of age, is in the Ursuline Convent at Quebec. I will return home immediately; and if I cannot remove her any other way, I will drag her out by the hair of her head, and raise a noise about their ears that shall not soon be quieted."

That gentleman did so return to Quebec, since which he has again visited New York; and he stated, that upon his arrival in Quebec, he went to the Convent, and instantly removed his daughter from the Ursuline Nunnery; from whom he ascertained, as far as she had been initiated into the mysteries, that Maria Monk's descriptions of Canadian Nunneries are most minutely and undeniably accurate.[62]

When Maria Monk made her escape from the nunnery, she took refuge in the house of a woman named Lavalliere on Elizabeth street in Montreal; it was the second or third door from the corner of what is commonly called "the Bishop's Church." Madame Lavalliere when interviewed afterward confirmed that Maria Monk did arrive at her house at the time specified by Maria Monk, and that she was wearing the usual habiliments of a Nun. She stated that Maria made herself known to her as an escaped Nun. Madame Lavalliere stated that she provided her with other clothing; Madame Lavalliere afterward carried the nun's garments back to the Hotel Dieu Nunnery.[63]

Maria Monk was pregnant by a Catholic priest when she escaped from the nunnery. It was her desire to save her child from certain death that prompted her escape from the convent. She knew that the common practice in the nunnery was for a priest to baptize the newborn child and then to hand the infant over to a nun, who would put her hand over the infant's mouth and nose until it was suffocated to death.

After Maria escaped and then gave birth, she traveled to Montreal with some Protestants who were assisting her in seeking justice in the courts. The entire time after her escape she never let the name of the Catholic priest who was the father of her child pass her lips.[64] When Catholic priest Patrick Phelan (1795-1857)[65] found out that Maria Monk was in Montreal and seeking prosecution for the tortures and murders in the nunnery, he made the following statement in front of the entire Catholic congregation after a Catholic Mass over which he was officiating:

> There is a certain nun in this city who has left our faith, and joined the Protestants. She has a child of which she is ready to swear I am the father. She wishes in this way to take my gown from me. If I knew where to find her, I would put her in prison. I mention this to guard you against being deceived by what she may say. The Devil now has such hold upon people that there is danger lest some might believe her story.[66]

There are two notable things about Phelan's statement: 1) He admits that Maria Monk was a nun (a fact that has always been denied by the Catholic hierarchy); and 2) He claimed that Maria was alleging that he was the father. In fact, Maria had not identified him as the father of her child. Maria had only stated that the father of her child was a Catholic priest, whom she never named. She stated that the nunnery was visited by scores of priests, who regularly entered the nunnery for illicit sex with the nuns. Maria agreed that Phelan was the father of her child only after word reached her of Phelan's statement made before the church congregation. Phelan made the statement before the church congregation, because his guilty conscience assumed that Maria had revealed him as the father. Logic tells us that a denial of a crime by a person before he is alleged to have committed it, suggests a guilty conscience by the denier. Only the most negligent officer of the law would not investigate the denier to determine whether the denial is a false cover for guilt. Phelan's denial under such a circumstance certainly points to him as the true father of Maria Monk's child, and as such confirms the truth of Maria Monk's other allegations.

   Samuel B. Smith, who was a former Catholic priest, published a booklet in 1836 titled, *Decisive Confirmation of the Awful Disclosures of Maria Monk*.[67] He knew that many of Maria Monk's claims are true, because when he was a Catholic priest, he was a superintendent of a nunnery in Kentucky. In an appendix to the second edition of Maria Monk's book, J. J. Slocum explains the importance of the opinion of Samuel B. Smith regarding the veracity of Maria Monk:

> Mr. Samuel B. Smith, who has been not only a Roman Priest, but has had several cages of nuns under his sole management,

questioned Maria Monk expressly respecting those affairs, customs, and ceremonies, which appertain only to nunneries, because they cannot be practiced by any other females but those who are shut up in those dungeons; and, after having minutely examined her, he plainly averred that it was manifest she could not have known the things which she communicated to him unless she had been a nun; not merely a scholar, or a temporary resident, or even a novice, but a nun, who had taken the veil, in the strictest sense of the appellative. This testimony is of the more value, because the conclusion does not depend upon any conflicting statements, of partial or prejudicial witnesses, but upon a fact which is essential to the system of monachism ; that no persons can know all the secrets of nunneries, but the Chaplain, the Abbess, and their accomplices in that "mystery of iniquity." Mr. Smith's declaration in one other respect is absolutely decisive. He has declared not only that Maria Monk has been a nun, but also that the descriptions which she gives are most minutely accurate.

Mr. Smith also testifies that the account which Maria Monk gives of the proceedings of the priests, the obscene questions which they ask young females, and their lewd practices with them at auricular confession, are constantly exemplified by the Roman Priests; and he also confirms her statements by the testimony of his own individual experience, and actual personal acquaintance with the Canadian nunneries, as well as with those in the United States, and especially of that at Monroe, Michigan, which was dissolved by Mr. Fenwick, on account of scandalous impurity, only about five years ago.[68]

The Catholic officials claimed that Maria Monk was never a Catholic nun. In his book, Samuel Smith reveals how he personally spoke with a witness who saw Maria Monk at the nunnery. The witness attended the congregational nunnery while she and Maria were only novices. The witness' family was able to get her out of the congregational nunnery after her brother when visiting her at the nunnery happened to see a priest put his arm around the neck of another nun and kiss her. This same witness was visiting an acquaintance in the publicly accessible area of the hospital that adjoined the black nunnery, when she saw Maria Monk serving the lunch. The witness was later determined to be Mrs. Hahn of Montreal.[69] Mrs. Hahn stated:

> I was born at Montreal, and resided there until within a few months, and where my friends still remain. I was educated among the Catholics, and have never separated myself from them.
>
> I knew Maria Monk when quite a child. We went to school together for about a year, as near as I can remember, to Mr. Workman,

Sacrament street, in Montreal. She is about one month younger than myself. We left that school at the same time, and entered the Congregational Nunnery nearly together. I could mention many things which I witnessed there, calculated to confirm some of her accounts.

I knew of the elopement of a priest named Leclere, who was a confessor, with a nun sent from the Congregational Nunnery, to teach in a village. They were brought back, after which she gave birth to an infant, and was again employed as a teacher.

Children were often punished in the Congregational Nunnery by being made to stand with arms extended, to imitate Christ's posture on the cross: and when we found vermin in our soup, as was often the case, we were exhorted to overcome our repugnance to it, because Christ died for us. I have seen such belts as are mentioned in the 'Awful Disclosures,' as well as gags; but never saw them applied

Maria Monk left the Congregational Nunnery before I did, and became a novice in the Hotel Dieu. I remember her entrance into the latter very well, for we had a '*jour de conge*,' holiday, on that occasion.

Some short time subsequently, after school hours one afternoon, while in the school room in the second story of the Congregational Nunnery, several of the girls standing near a window exclaimed, 'There is Maria Monk.' I sprang to the window to look, and saw with her several other novices, in the yard of the Hotel Dieu, among the plants which grew there. She did not appear to notice us, but I perfectly recognized her.

I have frequently visited the public hospital of the Hotel Dieu. It is the custom there (or some of the nuns and novices to enter at three o'clock P. M., in procession, with food and delicacies for the sick. I recollect some of my visits there by circumstances attending them. For instance, I was much struck, on several occasions, by the beauty of a young novice, whose slender, graceful form, and interesting appearance, distinguished her from the rest. On inquiry I learnt that her name was Dubois, or something like it, and the daughter of an old man who had removed from the country, and lived near the Place d'Armes. She was so generally admired for her beauty, that she was called 'la belle St. Francois' — St. Francis being the saint's name she had assumed in the convent. [**Editor's Note**: Saint Francis was a nun who was brutally stomped to death by the other nuns (with the assistance of five priests) upon the order of the Catholic Bishop and the Lady Superior. The reason for her execution was that another nun had informed the Lady Superior that Saint Francis stated that she wished to escape, she had firmly resolved to resist every attempt to compel her to commit detestable crimes, and that she would rather die than take part in the murder of newborn infants born to nuns in the Hotel Dieu Nunnery].

I frequently went to the hospital to see two of my particular friends who were novices; and subsequently to visit one who had a sore throat, and was sick for some weeks. I saw Maria Monk there many times, in the dress of a novice, employed in different ways; but we were never allowed to speak to each other.

Towards the close of the winter 1833-4, I visited the hospital of the Hotel Dieu very frequently, to see Miss Bourke, a friend of mine, although I was not allowed to speak with her. While there one day, at the hour of *'conge,'* collation, which, as I before stated was at three P. M., a procession of nuns and novices entered, and among the former I saw Maria Monk, with a black veil, &c. She perceived and recognized me; but put her finger upon her lips in toke of silence; and knowing how rigidly the rules were enforced, I did not speak.

A short time afterwards, I saw her again in the same place, and under similar circumstances.

I can fix the year when this occurred, because I recollect that the nuns in the hospital stared at a red dress I wore that season; and I am certain about the time of year, becaues I left my galo-shoes at the door before I went in.

The improper conduct of a priest was the cause of my leaving the Congregational Nunnery; for my brother saw him kissing a female one day while he was on a visit to me, and exclaimed—'O mon Dieu! what a place you are in—if father does not take you out of it, I will, if I have to tear you away.'

After the last sight I had of Maria Monk in the hospital, I never saw nor heard of her, until I had been an inhabitant for some time of New York. I then saw an extract from 'Awful Dislosures,' published in a newspaper, when I was perfectly satisfied that she was the authoress, and again at liberty. I was unable for several weeks to find her residence, but at length visited the house when she was absent. Seeing an infant among a number of persons who were strangers to me, as those present will testify, I declared that it must be the child mentioned in her book, from the striking resemblance to father Phelan, whom I well know.—This declaration has also been made by others.

> When Maria Monk entered, she passed across the room without turning toward me; but I recognized her by her gait, and when she saw me she knew me at once. I have since spent many hours with her, and am entirely convinced of the truth of her story, especially as I knew many things before, which tend to confirm the statements which she makes.[70]

Mrs. Hahn's averments were confirmed by another witness. The aforementioned architect stated that his daughter was a schoolmate with Maria Monk, and he and his wife knew Maria well. He stated that after Maria Monk took the veil of a novice, his daughter frequently saw Maria Monk wearing her novice's habit. His entire family knew personally that Maria Monk had taken the nun's veil and entered the Hotel Dieu Nunnery.[71]

The priests alleged that they had an affidavit from Maria Monk's mother that stated Maria was never in the nunnery. The purported affidavit from Maria Monk's mother does not bear her mother's signature. Maria Monk's mother wrote a letter to Maria, wherein she stated that she neither wrote nor signed the affidavit attributed to her. Maria's mother stated that she had been prevailed upon by the Catholic priests to allow it to go uncontradicted, but that it was written by someone else.[72] Maria's mother was known to be an alcoholic, who was putty in the manipulative hands of the Catholic priests and did not resist the priests efforts to destroy her daughter's credibility. The false affidavit prepared by the priests is impeached by what Maria's mother had told William Miller. Several years before Maria escaped, Maria's mother told a family friend, William Miller, that Maria was in the nunnery.

William Miller signed an affidavit under oath on March 3, 1836, stating that he knew Maria Monk when she was a child and attended school with her and her four brothers. He stated that his family and the Monk family were intimate friends, as his father had a high regard for Maria's father, Captain William Monk, who died suddenly from being poisoned. Miller stated that the "temper of his [Captain Monk's] wife was such, even at that time, as to cause much trouble."[73] In 1832, Miller left Montreal and moved to New York. He stated that "about a year afterward I visited Montreal, and on the day when the Governor reviewed the troops, I believe about the end of August, I called at the Government House, where I saw Mrs. Monk and several of the family. I inquired where Maria was, and she told me that she was in the nunnery."[74] Years later, after Maria's escape, Miller spoke with Maria and read her book. Miller concluded his sworn affidavit with: "I declare my personal knowledge of many facts stated in her book, and my full belief in the truth of her story, which, shocking as it is, cannot appear incredible to those persons acquainted with Canada."[75]

10 The Jesuit Scheme of Suborning Perjury

The Jesuits had other arrows in their quiver of deceit, and they shot them all at Maria Monk. The Jesuits were not going to confess guilt, and they could not allow the facts to be objectively examined, so they had to destroy the credibility of Maria Monk. They accomplished their goal only regarding the gullible masses. For those who examined closely the Jesuit evidence, it was apparent that it was completely manufactured.

Their efforts to destroy Maria Monk's credibility by assassinating her character have continued unabated to the present day. For example, the *Catholic Encyclopedia* lists Maria Monk among those the Catholic Church describes as "impostors." Included with Maria Monk by the *Catholic Encyclopedia* in the list of impostors is Charles Chiniquy. The Catholic Encyclopedia describes Maria Monk's book as being fueled by anti-Catholic prejudice, and implied that Maria was not a nun. The Catholic Encyclopedia claimed that Maria's account of the murders and immoralities inside the Hotel Dieu Nunnery had been "fully refuted from the very first by unimpeachable Protestant testimony, which proved that during the period of Maria Monk's alleged residence in the convent she was leading the life of a prostitute in the city."[76] Close scrutiny of the alleged "unimpeachable protestant evidence" shows it to be lacking in reliability, thin in substance, and not truly Protestant. The slightest wave of examination causes the smokescreen of deception to disappear, revealing behind it Jesuit priests fueling the illusion.

The Jesuits suborned perjury from loyal Catholics under their control. The Jesuits produced witnesses who claimed that Maria could not have been a nun in the Hotel Dieu Nunnery of Montreal, because, they alleged, she worked as a prostitute for two years from 1832 to 1834, prior to entering the Magdalen Asylum in November 1834. The Jesuit false witnesses described Maria Monk during that period as having displaying "confirmed vagrancy," "strange frightiness and unaccountable irregularities," "insanity," "thievery,""lies," and "profligacy."[77]

The Jesuits were firing their arrows of deceit so haphazardly that they ended up shooting their own witnesses. One set of false witnesses contradicted other false witnesses. The Jesuits produced a different set of witnesses who alternatively claimed that for 15 months, from the spring of 1833 until July 1834, Maria was employed as a school teacher. The Jesuits would have people believe that Maria's employers were so derelict that they never noticed that the teacher they had hired to teach their children was an obviously insane, thieving, prostitute.[78]

The Jesuits had to account for the entire time Maria spent in the Hotel Dieu Nunnery. They desperately scraped the bottom of the societal barrel to find false witnesses who claimed that Maria Monk was employed as a servant girl in the Gouin family household from November 1831 until September 1832 in the small Canadian town of Sorel.[79] However, the witnesses that the Jesuits put forth were completely lacking in credibility. Charles Gouin was one of the Jesuit witnesses. Protestant minister J.J. Slocum summarized the character (or rather lack-thereof) of Charles Gouin: "Mr. Gouin is stated, by very respectable authority, to be a Roman Catholic, so far as he has any religion. A man notoriously destitute of moral principle; a bankrupt, owing much and paying little. He is described by his own friends, as 'an active conspirator, unworthy of confidence.'"[80]

Another false witness to Maria Monk's presence in Sorel as a servant girl was Mary Angelica Monk, who was no relation to Maria Monk. Pastor Slocum says of the character of that witness: "She is an impure woman; having been separated from her husband, on the ground of her criminal connection with a man by the name of Hall. Report also says, that she is very intimate with the notoriously profligate priest Kelly, of Sorel."[81]

The third witness in this trinity of deceit was one Martel Paul Hus Cournoier. J.J. Slocum reveals the character of Cournier.

> The affidavit of this man has every appearance of having been fabricated, for the sole purpose of bolstering up, not only the testimony of Mr. Gouin and Mrs. [Mary

Angelica] Monk, but also that of other individuals, to be examined hereafter. He is described by those who know him, "as an illiterate fellow, who can neither read nor write; an active speculator, of no property, little credit, reputation for virtue or integrity; having not long since debauched one of his own creed named Couthnay." He was convicted of perjury in the case of the King against Isaac Jones and others, for the murder of Louis Marcoux. If any man in Canada doubts the truth of this, he is referred to the legal registers of that Province, for the proof of it. Such, then, is the unprincipled character of Martel Paul: and I ask, what confidence can be reposed in the affidavit of such a perjured ignoramus?[82]

These witnesses alleged that for the ten months from November 1831 until September 1832, Maria Monk could not have been in the Hotel Dieu Nunnery, as Maria claimed, because she was working as a servant girl in the Gouin household in Sorel. The town of Sorel is on the banks of the St. Lawrence River, and at the time in 1832 only had fifteen hundred residents. In small towns during the 1800's, with no television or internet, social intercourse was much greater than it is today. Everybody knew everybody else living in small towns. Think about that. In that entire town of fifteen hundred people, the Jesuit priests could only produce a convicted perjurer, an adulterer, and a bankrupt as their star witnesses to prove that Maria Monk was in Sorel and not in the Hotel Dieu Nunnery.

Maria Monk claimed that she had never been to Sorel. If Maria was not in the town of Sorel, it should be easy enough to establish by asking any of the remaining residents of Sorel. Pastor Slocum did just that. He determined that Maria Monk was telling the truth when she averred that she had never lived in Sorel, as was falsely claimed by the Jesuit priests. Pastor Slocum presents the testimony of a reputable merchant in Sorel, who lived near the home where Maria Monk was allegedly employed as servant girl.

> Mr. Buttery declared, that it was impossible for her [Maria Monk] to have resided in Sorel, as above stated, without his having had some knowledge of it. He was, therefore, decidedly of the opinion that she had never lived in that place. Mr. Buttery lives near Mr. Gouin's, And would of course have seen her, had she lived there for ten months.[83]

Pastor Slocum found a second witness, John Edler, who resided in Sorel and was often in the home of the Gouin's, where Maria Monk was alleged to have been employed as a servant girl. Mr. Edler states without equivocation that Maria Monk was not a servant girl in the Gouin home and was not a resident of Sorel as alleged by the Jesuit priests.

> The following testimony of Mr. John Edler, of New York, is decisive on the point. Mr. Edler first became acquainted with Maria Monk some time in the summer of 1836, in the city of New York. His statement is as

follows: "I have friends, a grand-parent and a brother, residing in Sorel or William Henry, whom I have frequently visited in that place. My mother resided there before her decease. I am personally acquainted with Mr. Charles Gouin and his family, who keep a tavern in Sorel. Their residence is in the immediate vicinity of my relatives. On one occasion I resided with my connections in Sorel, for about the space of nine months, immediately preceding the commencement of the Cholera in July, 1832. During this period I was often at Mr. Gouin's, and personally knew the members of his household; and I am very certain that Maria Monk, authoress of the "Awful Disclosures," was not, during this period of time, a member of Mr. Gouin's family, in any sense whatever. Nor did I ever hear of her living in Sorel, until I recently heard of it in New York. I first became acquainted with Maria Monk in New York, some three or four months since." Mr. Edler's testimony covers eight out of the ten months, during which time, Mr. Gouin says, that Maria Monk was a menial in his family. Mr. Edler, so far as I have been able to ascertain, is a young gentleman of veracity and industry. His statement, therefore, can be relied on as true. Since writing the above, a lady from Sorel has visited Maria Monk in New York. And she gives it as her decided opinion, that the authoress of the "Awful Disclosures" has never been a resident of Sorel, as testified by the priests' witnesses. Thus the evidence, that Charles Gouin, Mariel Paul Hus Cournoier, and Angelica Monk have given false testimony, is constantly augmenting. It is evident, therefore, that Maria Monk, authoress of the "Awful Disclosures," has not resided in Sorel, as maintained by the priests and their perjured supporters.[84]

11 Mental Reservation

How is it that the Jesuits could so easily persuade someone to lie on their behalf? It is a Roman Catholic doctrine that has been the centuries-old ethic of the Catholic Church that it is permissible to lie in order to protect the Roman Catholic Church from scandal. The Jesuits permit the use of ambiguous terms to mislead a judge or outright lying under oath if the witness makes a mental reservation.[85] The Jesuits are so famous for deception that the term "Jesuitical" is defined in the Oxford Dictionary as: "Dissembling or equivocating, in the manner once associated with Jesuits."[86] Noah Webster's 1828 dictionary defines Jesuitical as: "Designing; cunning; deceitful; prevaricating."[87]

The Jesuits, and indeed all Catholic priestly orders, not only teach that it is permissible to lie to protect the Catholic Church from scandal, they have also devised a method for deception that persuades Catholics to lie who would otherwise be reticent to lie. The artifice of deception used by the priests is called "mental reservation."

Catholic priests teach that if one makes a mental reservation when telling a lie, the lie is not technically a lie. The Jesuits teach that it is not a sin if one silently, to himself, adds some qualification to the lying words he speaks. The Catholic priests teach that if the unspoken thought, when added to the spoken words, make the statement technically true, then it is not technically a lie.

For instance, hypothetically, a priest or nun could say falsely that Maria Monk was never a nun at the Hotel Dieu Nunnery, and make a mental reservation, thinking silently to themselves the words "prior to 1800." The mental reservation of "prior to 1800" if they were spoken would make the statement technically true, but the words are not spoken, and the listener does not hear the mental reservation. The listener only hears the false denial. According to the Catholic ethic, however, the mental reservation by the speaker makes his statement technically true and therefore not a lie, even though the spoken words that are heard are not true. It is this deceitful Jesuitical cunning that has required the U.S. Government to add to oaths and affirmations a clause that the person makes the affirmation "without any mental reservation or purpose of evasion."

Indeed, this Catholic ethic allowing mental reservation is still taught and practiced today. The Catholic ethic of mental reservation has become an issue in litigation over the rape of young children by Catholic priests. In one 2007 lawsuit in California, an elderly nun, under questioning by a lawyer, made statements that were inconsistent with the known facts. The lawyer was suspicious about her answers and asked her whether she subscribed to the practice of making "mental reservations." John Spano, reported for *The Los Angeles Times* that the lawyer "asked whether she was familiar with 'mental reservation'—a 700-year-old doctrine by which clerics may avoid telling the truth to protect the Catholic Church. She explained in her own way that it is 'to protect the church from scandal.' She said she subscribed to the doctrine."[88]

Spano reported that at least a half-dozen lawyers representing victims in sex abuse cases against priests in the Los Angeles Archdiocese have encountered Catholic witnesses using mental reservation as a means of deception.[89] Spano explained: "The doctrine has been used in modern times to 'claim that it is morally justifiable to lie in order to protect the reputation of the institutional church,' said Thomas P. Doyle, a Virginia priest who is an expert in canon law and has been widely consulted by lawyers for people who say they were victims of abuse."[90]

The lawyers representing the Catholic Church clearly understand the implications of bringing up the topic of mental reservation. The lawyers typically object to any discussion of the topic. Spano gives one instance: "A lawyer preparing one of the more than 500 claims of abuse against the Roman Catholic Archdiocese of Los Angeles asked a priest giving a sworn statement the same question [about making a mental reservation] earlier this month. His lawyer quickly intervened, telling the priest not to answer."[91] The lawyers representing the Roman Catholic Church are trying to avoid the type of answer given by a priest to Tim Hale, who is an attorney for victims of pedophile priests. Hale stated "that one priest answered yes without hesitation when asked if mental reservation 'is a doctrine that protects the church from scandal.'"[92]

12 Mass Graves

Charlotte Keckler's (a/k/a Charlotte Wells) (1889-1983) account of her experience in a cloistered nunnery adds further corroboration of Maria Monk's account. Charlotte Keckler wrote an exposé revealing torture and abuse that she suffered during the twenty two years she spent in a cloistered convent.[93] She initially entered into the convent voluntarily thinking that she would be serving the Lord Jesus, but soon found that she was serving the very church of the devil. Once she became a cloistered nun, she found that she was imprisoned with no way out. After twenty-two years she finally found an opportunity and made her escape. Charlotte revealed that the Catholic priests use the cloistered convents as private brothels. The nuns often became pregnant from fornicating with the Catholic priests. Upon giving birth, the newborn baby is murdered.

Charlotte Keckler stated:

Many have said I exaggerate and that these

things are not so, but I have yet to be hauled into court to refute the charges. They would have to open the cloisters and this they dare not do. After being snared in this rotten system for twenty-two years, I know whereof I speak. Normal young expectant mothers eagerly anticipate the arrival of their precious baby. Everything is ready, nursery, crib, clothing, and everyone is happy with her. By contrast, a little nun in the convent dreads the moment when she gives birth. The child is the product of a shameful, illicit union with a drunken priest which was forced on her. She knows from bitter experience that the baby will only be permitted to live four or five hours at the very most. It will never be cleaned or wrapped in a warm blanket for Mother Superior will put her hand over its mouth and pinch its nostrils to snuff out its life.

This is why there are lime pits in all the convents. Babies' bodies are tossed in these holes to be destroyed. Pray for the government to force the convents to open their doors to release the prisoners and let the whole world see what horrors are hidden behind those doors of cruel religious hypocrisy.

If this happens, I assure you that even the Catholic people will agree to the closing of the convents as they did in Mexico in 1934. They have no idea what is transpiring there either, or they would never expose their daughters to such barbarous debauchery and torture.

The convents in old Mexico have been turned into government museums which you can tour for a modest fee. You should go and see with your own eyes and touch with your hands the things of which I speak. Go down into the dungeons, through the tunnels and torture chambers and see all the fiendish devices, demonically conceived, to inflict suffering on the bodies of helpless nuns. See for yourself the cells in which nuns were locked each night and examine the beds, and the prayer boards.[94]

Mass graves for murdered infants of nuns are a common feature in and around convents and have been uncovered in other countries. Former Jesuit priest, Alberto Rivera, revealed that frequently there are underground tunnels that link seminaries for priests with convents for nuns that facilitated the secret fornication between the nuns and priests. Rivera revealed that many mass grave sites for infants born to nuns and shortly thereafter murdered were discovered in Spain and Rome in and around convents and seminaries.[95] Infanticide is part of the overriding ethic of the Jesuits that the ends justify the means. The Jesuits believe that if one can get away with committing a crime without getting caught, it ceases to be a crime. Indeed, F. Xavier Makami, Prefect at the Jesuit College at Ro jen wrote that "successful crime ceases to be a crime. Success constitutes or absolves the guilty at its will."[96] Infanticide is justified by Jesuit theologians. Julia McNair Wright cites

Jesuit authorities who justify infanticide, in order to protect the Roman church from scandal: "For the sake of concealing infamy and preserving reputations, infanticide is not only permitted but enjoined by Ariault in his propositions; by Marin, Theology, Tract 23; Castro Palms; Egidius; Bannez; Henriquez; and many other Jesuits."[97] Pastor J. J. Slocum quotes the writings of Hulderic, who states that "Pope Gregory, drawing his fishpond, found more than six thousand heads of infants in it; upon which he deeply repented, and, confessing that the decree of unnatural celibacy was the cause of so horrid a slaughter, he condemned it, adding: 'It is better to marry than to give occasion of death.'"[98]

The Roman Catholic Church has a long and sordid history of secretly disposing in mass graves those who die under suspicious circumstances. In 1993, a mass grave containing 133 bodies was uncovered on the grounds of a previously closed Roman Catholic Magdalene laundry run at a nunnery north of Dublin, Ireland.[99] The so-called Magdalene Laundries were run by nuns and housed young girls, who were held in involuntary servitude. Many of the girls had died in the 1960s and 1970s. All of the remains found in the mass grave were girls who had died in the laundry, but the Roman Catholic Church could not identify 45 of the remains, and 80 of the deceased did not have death certificates as required by law. As the exhumation continued, 22 additional bodies were found making for a total of 155 bodies unearthed; who knows how many other bodies are buried in secret graves elsewhere on the property.

It is illegal in Ireland (and indeed almost every other civilized country) not to notify the government of a death occurring on your premises. The fact that the Catholic nunnery did not report the deaths suggests that they did not want the evidence of the cause of death, which would be manifested on the body, to be known by the authorities. The nunnery clearly had something to hide.

If a grave with the remains of a single unreported death were found on the property of an ordinary private citizen, there would be an immediate investigation, and it would become widely circulated news. The homeowner would be the focus of an unrelenting investigation into the cause of death. Those same rules do not apply to the Roman Catholic Church. The power of the Catholic Church is so absolute in Ireland that there has been no investigation into how the girls died, nor has there been (at the very least) an inquiry into why the Catholic Church did not report the deaths, as required by law.

13 Captive Prisoners

William Stone made the absurd statement that Maria Monk is not to be believed, because she had no need to escape from the nunnery, as she was free to leave at any time. Stone stated: "But whence this great difficulty of escaping? There are plenty of doors and gates, and every nun has a key at her side."[100] Anyone who knows anything about cloistered nunneries could see through Stone's bold-faced lie. The very fact that the only former cloistered nuns who have ever left a nunnery have done so by escaping is testimony that nuns in cloistered nunneries are not free to leave and in fact are kept as prisoners.

Former cloistered nun, Charlotte Wells (real name: Charlotte Keckler), escaped her captivity. Prior to her death in 1983, she stated the following, which refutes the claim by the priests that the nuns can leave the cloistered nunnery at any time.

No one imprisoned behind those walls ever

comes out to tell the awful story. Priests will glibly pooh, pooh the idea that there is anything amiss. They will tell you that in this country and elsewhere sisters can walk out of the convents anytime they please. That is a lie! I was shut up for twenty-two years and tried everything to escape. I even carried tablespoons to the dungeons and desperately dug in their dirt floors attempting to find a way out. Why a tablespoon? All the other tools were locked up or carefully supervised. They were used to dig the tunnels and underground chambers. Convents are constructed like prisons to thwart the escape of the nuns.[101]

Cloistered nuns are kept prisoner. They can never leave the nunnery. Once they agree to enter the cloister, their decision is irrevocable. Many of the poor nuns change their minds after realizing that they have entered into a hellish life of abuse, rape, torture, and murder. However, they are not allowed to leave.

For example, after taking her vows as a nun in 1854, Josephine Bunkley came to realize that she had been hoodwinked and had made a terrible mistake by entering the convent. However, once the door was shut and barred behind her, she was not free to leave; she was literally a captive, held in involuntary servitude. That is notable since the order she joined, "Sisters of Charity," is not, strictly speaking, a cloistered community. Miss Bunkley's experience reveals that even supposed open orders like the "Sisters of Charity" require forced confinement for at least some of their nuns. Miss Bunkley realized that the only way for her to get free was to surreptitiously escape. She ultimately escaped and revealed to the world the slavish conditions in the convent.

The nuns in St. Joseph's convent were mistreated and literally worked to death. The poor nuns were so malnourished and overworked under such spartan conditions that their frail constitutions and compromised immune systems could not fight off disease. During the ten months of her stay in the convent, Miss Bunkley witnessed the deaths of 14 nuns.[102] Lest dear reader you think that this is an exaggeration, on December 1, 1854, the mother superior of St. Joseph's convent wrote a letter that was published in a local newspaper, in which she acknowledged the high mortality rate at the convent. Her letter was intended to refute the claims of austere abuse leveled by Josephine Bunkley. The mother superior, Etienne Hall, Jesuitically claimed that the high death rate of the nuns was not caused by their wasting away in slow despair while imprisoned in the convent, but rather by their self-sacrificing attendance to the ill, whose diseases they caught, thus causing their death.[103]

The mother superior, in her letter to the editor, further claimed that the nuns were all free to leave the convent at any time. Miss Bunkley responded to the mother superiors' "myth" of freedom enjoyed by the nuns:

> I would ask in the name of charity and sound reason, can any plausible motive be assigned why I should escape from the institution, at a risk of detection and punishment, and travel ten miles on an unknown road, exposed to danger and

insult, if I enjoyed the privilege of departure at free choice? Until a rational motive be adduced, is there not a fair presumption, at least, that I have spoken the truth?[104]

Ordinarily prisons are to punish the guilty. Cloistered nunneries are the reverse; they are prisons where the guilty mete out punishment to the innocent. Miss Bunkley further pointed out that if the nuns are free to leave their nunneries, as claimed by the mother superior, why are dead bolts, bars, gratings, and high walls invariable and essential characteristics of nunneries?[105] Indeed, nunneries are the perfect fortress hideouts for the Catholic priesthood to satisfy their lecherous lusts and avaricious greed.

Mother Superior Etienne Hall's claim that nuns are free to leave, contradicts several canonized "saints" of the Catholic Church. One of those "saints" is Alphonsus Liguori. He is one of the most authoritative of Catholic writers on the doctrines and practices of the monastic orders. Liguori asks "what ought a person to do who finds that she has become a nun against her inclination?"[106] His response is that since she is now in a nunnery she should stay. Liguori acknowledges in his answer that she has been "placed in the house of God (either voluntarily or unwillingly) the spouse of Jesus Christ." It matters not to Liguori that the poor nun is confined unwillingly. Liguori states that he has no pity for the nun who is confined, even against her will, because he likens the confinement in the nunnery as a "healthful country" and the outside world by comparison is "infected with pestilence, and surrounded by enemies."[107] Liguori argues that, in essence, the nun should be thankful for her involuntary imprisonment, because in his view it is better than being in the outside world.

Liguori states the official Catholic doctrine. Liguori could not be clearer, Catholic doctrine sanctions the involuntary confinement of nuns. Liguori assumes in his writings that it is impossible for the nun who no longer wishes to be a nun to leave the convent. Consequently, according to Liguori, she has only two choices in her imprisonment: 1) be miserable or 2) be cheerful. Liguouri's advice to the imprisoned nun is to "make a virtue of necessity" and pass her involuntary confinement with cheerfulness, otherwise she will be miserable on earth and be damned to hell for eternity.

> [N]ow that you are professed in a convent, and it is IMPOSSIBLE FOR YOU TO LEAVE IT, tell me what do you wish to do? If you have entered religion [i.e. become a nun] against your inclination, you must remain with cheerfulness. If you abandon yourself to melancholy, you must lead a life of misery, and will expose yourself to great danger of suffering *a hell here,* and another hereafter. YOU MUST THEN MAKE A VIRTUE OF NECESSITY.[108] (small caps, block parenthesis, and italics in original)

The principle expounded by the Catholic "saint" and followed in the Catholic nunneries worldwide is that a confined nun should not hope to leave the nunnery because "it is impossible to for you to leave it." Instead, she must "make a virtue" of her stay in her cloistered prison.

It has been the common practice for a young girl to be forced into a nunnery by her deluded Catholic family. What is the Catholic doctrine in such a case? We are not left guessing. We can rely on the authoritative pronouncements of another Catholic saint, Francis de Sales. He founded the Catholic priestly order of the Oblates of St. Francis de Sales (Latin: Oblati Sancti Francisci Salesii, O.S.F.S.). They are affiliated with the Oblate Sisters of St. Francis de Sales. Francis de Sales also founded an order of cloistered nuns, called the Order of the Visitation of Holy Mary. Not surprisingly, Francis de Sales wholeheartedly approved of the practice of Catholic families forcing their daughters into involuntary confinement in a cloistered nunnery. Lewis Hippolytus and Joseph Tonna explain:

> Being asked his opinion regarding a person who had *become a nun against her will*, St. Francis de Sales answered: "It is true that *this child, if she had not been obliged by her parents, would not have left the world; but this is of little importance, provided she knows that the* FORCE *employed by her parents is more useful to her than* the permission to follow her own will. For now she can say: If I had not lost such liberty, I should have lost true liberty." The saint (!) meant to say, that had she not *been compelled by her parents to become a nun*, her liberty, which would have induced her to remain in the world, would have robbed her of the true liberty of the children of God, which consists in freedom from the chains and dangers in this world.[109] (italics,

small caps, and parenthetical in original)

The life of a former nun known only as Coralla, was narrated by her in several chapters in a book published in 1855. Coralla explained the subtle tactics used to inveigle young girls into taking the vows of a nun in a cloistered convent. It is often the case that the Catholic Church seeks to steal the inheritance of a wealthy girl. Once the rich girl takes the vow of poverty, she is then compelled under that oath to sign over all of her earthly belongings to the Catholic Church. The poor girl is then held a miserable prisoner in the convent. She is given a life sentence of imprisonment behind the walls of a nunnery; her only fault was being born rich and innocent of the wiles of the Catholic Church.

> Some of them had been inveigled there by false pretenses, and then incarcerated at the desire of persons who wished to obtain their property. This is a very common thing, as I have reason to believe, in other parts of Italy, and in all other countries where convents exist. No two cases may be exactly alike; but many resemble each other in this, that a helpless girl is made the victim of the avarice of some person or persons in or out of the convent. The bishop or other ecclesiastic, secretly ascertains the amount and position of her expected estate, and then resorts to every possible means to obtain it. If she is accessible to the influence of any of his spies or emissaries, he sends to her an insidious agent, in the shape of a confessor,

an applicant for charity, a servant, a teacher of music, a gentleman of pleasing manners, who flatters her with his attentions, or a grave and courteous lady, of middle age, who expresses a great and motherly interest in her trials and her pleasures. She is gradually drawn towards the convent, as a visitor, and there finds impressive scenes prepared for her, which are carefully adapted to her peculiar character or state of mind.[110]

No doubt, the target of the Catholic plot will have friends who are not quite as naive of the stratagems of the Catholic Church and will seek to warn her of the danger. The Catholic Church has nefarious ways of removing such an impediment to its avarice.

If any friend is likely to oppose obstacles in the way of bringing a victim into a convent, any necessary expedient is resorted to, to prevent and counteract his influence. False reports are raised against a father, an uncle, a brother, or a guardian, by "which his character is injured, his business impaired or ruined, his courage is overcome. He is prosecuted for debt, by some one who has lent him money, or made a contract with him for that express purpose; he is, perhaps, written to from a distance, to make a journey on business, for pleasure, or for the comfort of some person in distress, and is detained or imprisoned far from home; or wounded or killed on the

> road. The Inquisition has often given its assistance in cases of this kind; and the father or friend most disposed to defeat the designs of the rapacious persecutor of a young heiress, has, in many instances, been denounced by an unknown accuser, and then seized at midnight by a band of familiars, "*in the name of the Holy Office*," put into a secret dungeon, never to be heard of again, until the sound of the last trumpet.[111] (italics in original)

Often, there is a feigned friend or family insider who takes part in the conspiracy with Catholic clerics to inveigle an unsuspecting girl into a nunnery. He does so upon the motive of taking his share of the loot.

> It sometimes happens that more than one person is concerned in the enterprise, who agree and share in the plunder of the property taken from the victim. A priest and a lawyer, or a profligate relation, or family friend, combine their infernal arts, and afterwards divide the spoil. As every nun is required to renounce her worldly possessions, under the fiction of giving herself to the service of God, devoting her life to the saving of her soul, and being "married to Jesus Christ," she is regarded by the civil laws of Popish countries, as well as by the canon law of Rome, as having no power to hold property, and her estate goes to her husband the church. It is taken from her control and possession, and

nominally given to the convent, but usually, in whole or in part, in some way or other, is so disposed of, that it passes into the hands of her robbers. When too late, the poor girl, though born and reared in comfort, abundance, or perhaps, in the highest ranks of opulent society, soon finds herself left to sink to the degraded level of common nuns.[112]

Another cause of a young girl being imprisoned in a nunnery is the superstitious belief of her Catholic parents. Motivated by religious zeal, the deluded parents are convinced by the Catholic priest that their daughter can become a saint through her monastic efforts. Furthermore, they believe that in her worship before the throne of God, she can help ensure the entrance of her family into heaven. The parents are deceived by priests and nuns into believing that their daughter will be living a life of spiritual joy. They are, however, completely unaware of the hellish enslavement that awaits their innocent daughter. The parents do not know that their letters are intercepted by the mother superior and responses to those letters are dictated by the mother superior to the nun to write back to her parents. In those letters, the poor nun falsely assures them that she is perfectly happy and has no interest in leaving the nunnery; when, in fact, she is miserably imprisoned and often wishes for death to hasten an end to her wretchedness. Coralla states:

> I have often felt the strongest desire to remonstrate with parents, and especially mothers, on the injustice and cruelty of sending their daughters to nunneries. Could

they see what I have seen, they never would take such a step; could they have felt what I have heard others express, and what I have known by my own experience, nothing on earth could ever induce one of them to permit a child so much as to approach a convent, or hold any intercourse with the priests or their emissaries, who go about to inveigle the inexperienced and unsuspecting. Many a fond parent, who has a daughter in a convent, deceives herself with the hope that her child is happy, in the enjoyment of a holy seclusion, safe from the temptations and dangers of the world. She confides in the promises made, and the assurances given, thinking that all must be right, and that everything is as it seems. How sad is generally the reverse, how different is the tale which the poor girl would tell, if allowed, as she ought to be, to speak the truth freely![113]

Coralla describes a convent as a place of perfect misery and degradation.

I know enough, however, to be assured that the convent was a place of misery, a perfect prison, and house of punishment, and I might say of torture, moral and mental. So I am sure almost every nun would have declared, if allowed the freedom of speech; and I am confident that every one would have been glad to leave it in a moment, if she had known of any place of refuge, and

> secured from the dreadful severity of the laws, which, to the imagination of the poor, timid nun, always hang, like a dark thunder-cloud, all round the convent outside of the walls. And to her everything beyond is gloom, danger, and fear. Her friends, if she ever had any, she has renounced, or they have renounced her; and there is not a ray of hope, not a way of escape, or a place of refuge on earth.[114]

Coralla explains how the priests, like foxes overseeing a henhouse, use the nunnery as their personal brothel. They use their position of authority to seduce the innocence from the nuns.

> I could tell mothers what I can only intimate to others. I could show them that their daughters would be exposed to any treatment to which the men who have control within the walls might choose to subject them, and those men, often the most degraded and vicious of the human race, trained to iniquity, accustomed to hear sin justified by false reasoning under the cloak of religion, and encouraged by the general example of others, and emboldened by the entire secresy [*sic*] which they can draw around them. Such are bishops and priests; and, as they have power to remove and replace the Superiors of convents, and control over the old nuns, who are the officers under her, there is nothing wanting to render a nunnery, such as I have known,

not only an unfit place for a virtuous young woman, but the most unfit on earth. Parents! Parents! How can you be so blind to the worst enemies of your daughters?[115]

Once a nun takes her vows in a cloistered nunnery, she can never leave. The above quoted doctrines from Liguori and de Sales remain the official principles of cloistered nunneries today and authoritatively announce to the world that a nun may never leave the cloister. It has been Rome's boast for centuries that she never changes. The cloistered prisons of popish superstition remain today. In 2007, Diane Sawyer interviewed Mother Mary Francis, who was the mother superior at the cloistered convent of the Poor Clares order in Roswell, New Mexico. The mother superior told Diane Sawyer that the nuns "ordinarily" never leave the convent. In a voice-over, Diane Sawyer describes the cloistered nunnery and the ceremony of solemn vows and asks: "After this moment, what if you change your mind? Can you ever leave? What if you change your mind?" That voice-over question led into an interview with the mother superior, where she was asked by Diane Sawyer if "after you have taken the solemn perpetual vow can you then come in and say: 'not for me?'"[116] The mother superior, without hesitation, answered with an unequivocal "No," while emphatically shaking her head back and forth. The mother superior then added, "that would be a tragedy."[117]

The above program was posted on ABC's website. However, that part of the interview with the negative response from the mother superior was not part of the posting. The mother superior's response can only be viewed in a grainy duplicate on You Tube. Diane Sawyer seemed to have lost all curiosity after the mother superior's response. The mother superior's answer screams for a follow-up question, such as: "Would you use force to prevent a nun from leaving?" The implication from the mother superior's initial answer (although it was not said) is that force would be used to prevent a nun from leaving. Using force or the threat of force to keep someone confined against her will constitutes the crime of false imprisonment.

Diane Sawyer explained that when the nuns take their vow to enter the cloistered nunnery, they do so during a ceremony where they are portrayed as the bride of Christ. To leave the nunnery is theologically considered to be the equivalent of leaving their husband, Jesus Christ. Diane Sawyer explained in a voice-over that "we were told the spiritual consequences of leaving are considered dire, and in fact only the pope can give permission to dissolve marriage between a nun and Jesus."[118] So much for William Stone's incredible claim that the cloistered nuns are free to leave the convent at their will.

The priests consider themselves, *alter-Christos* (another Christ). They believe that they are in place of Christ on earth. According to their twisted theology, the priests are consummating the marriage between Christ and the nuns when they sexually assault the nuns in the convent.

14 Above the Law

In 1852, a movement was begun in Great Britain to petition the Parliament to provide for some means of inspecting convents to ensure that they are habitable and safe and that the nuns are not being held against their will.[119]

The Catholic Institute of Great Britain printed a pamphlet in response to the movement. Amazingly, the Catholic Institute actually tried to justify holding someone against her will in a convent. The Catholic pamphlet stated:

> Under our free government, are we not ourselves living in perpetual restraint? Is not our liberty curtailed and limited by many prohibitions and laws? Are not our soldiers bound by an irrevocable engagement as soon as they are enlisted, by which single act almost always done from want, or in a frolic, or in a state of intoxication are they not subject to a

discipline a thousand times more severe than that of the most rigid religious orders? Are they not, in truth, merely passive instruments in the hands of their commanding officers? Are not their diet, their sleep, their dress, even their motions, under continual restrictions? Willing or unwilling, are they not doomed to go wherever they are sent, even to the extremities of the world, and to the most unwholesome climates, to fight the battles of their country, with scarcely a hope of seeing their friends again in their native land?[120]

The Catholic Institute implicitly parallels the trickery used to inveigle boys into the military (which is described as: "want, or in a frolic, or in a state of intoxication") with the trickery used on girls to inveigle them into a nunnery, suggesting that is the way of the world, and it is as it should be.

The assumption of the Catholic Institute was that the Roman Catholic Church is equivalent in stature and function to the state. Just as the state can hold soldiers to service once entered against their will, so also may the Catholic Church hold nuns to service against their will.

Indeed, the very ritual performed upon becoming a nun testifies to the perpetual and insoluble service to which the nun is entering. She is simply not allowed out of her vows of poverty, chastity, and obedience. If she changes her mind, she is considered cursed, and she is held captive against her will. A terrible curse is heaped upon the nun and anyone who should assist her in her escape. The ritual curse announced during the induction ceremony is as follows:

> By the authority of Almighty God and his holy apostles Peter and Paul, we solemnly forbid, under pain of anathema, that any one draw away these present virgins, or holy nuns, from the divine service to which they have devoted themselves under the banner of chastity; or that any one purloin their goods, or hinder their possessing them unmolested; but if any one shall dare to attempt such a thing, let him be accursed at home and abroad; accursed in the city and in the field; accursed in waking and sleeping; accursed in eating and drinking; accursed in walking and sitting; cursed in his flesh and his bones; and from the sole of his foot to the crown of his head let him have no soundness. Come upon him the malediction which, by Moses in the Law, the Lord hath laid on the sons of iniquity. Be his name blotted out from the book of the living, and not be written with the righteous. His portion and inheritance be with Cain the fratricide, with Dathan and Abiram, with Ananias and Sapphira, with Simon the sorcerer, and with Judas the traitor, and with those who have said to God, 'Depart from us, we desire not the knowledge of thy ways.' Let him perish in the day of judgment, and let everlasting fire devour him, with the devil and his angels,

unless he make restitution and come to amendment. Fiat. Fiat. So be it. So be it.[121]

It is this fearful curse that frequently makes the family of an escaped nun zealous in advocating for her return. It is sometimes the case where secret arrangements are made between the church and the deluded superstitious family to return the escaped nun to captivity in the nunnery.

Indeed, the inviolability of all Catholic nunneries and monasteries is memorialized by the Council of Trent, which remains the official doctrine of the Roman Catholic Church.

> The holy Synod, renewing the constitution of Boniface VIII., which begins Periculoso, enjoins on all bishops, by the judgment of God to which It appeals, and under pain of eternal malediction, that, by their ordinary authority, in all monasteries subject to them, and in others, by the authority of the Apostolic See, they make it their especial care, that the enclosure of nuns be carefully restored, wheresoever it has been violated, and that it be preserved, wheresoever it has not been violated; repressing, by ecclesiastical censures and other penalties, without regarding any appeal whatsoever, the disobedient and gainsayers, and calling in for this end, if need be, the aid of the Secular arm. The holy Synod exhorts Christian princes to furnish this aid, and enjoins, under pain of excommunication, to

be ipso facto incurred, that it be rendered by all civil magistrates. But for **no nun, after her profession, shall it be lawful to go out of her convent, even for a brief period, under any pretext whatever**, except for some lawful cause, which is to be approved of by the bishop; any indults and privileges whatsoever notwithstanding. Council of Trent, Session 25, December 4, 1558, Chapter V (emphasis added).

The Council of Trent has in mind severe punishment for any nun or monk who should decide to leave his or her order. Many escaped nuns and monks have testified to the severe tortures that were endemic within the walls of their monasteries. The severest tortures are reserved for those who have escaped and been caught. Those tortures are authorized by the Council of Trent.

No Regular soever, who shall pretend that he entered into a religious order through compulsion and fear; or shall even allege that he made his profession before the proper age; or the like; and would fain lay aside his habit, be the cause what it may; or would even withdraw with his habit without the permission of his superior; shall be listened to, unless it be within five years only from the day of his profession, and not then either, unless he has produced before his own superior, and the Ordinary, the reasons which he alleges. But **if, before doing this, he has of his own accord laid aside his habit; he shall in no wise be**

admitted to allege any cause whatever; but shall be compelled to return to his monastery, and be punished as an apostate; and meanwhile he shall not have the benefit of any privilege of his order. Council of Trent, Session 25, December 4, 1558, Chapter XIX (emphasis added).

The Council of Trent provides that the penalty for escaping from a nunnery is to be **"punished as an apostate; and meanwhile he shall not have the benefit of any privilege of his order."** Please understand, dear reader, what it means not to have the benefit of any privilege of his order. A cloistered nun or monk is under an oath of obedience. To remove a privilege of the order is to compel the victim to forced incarceration without regard to their obedience. To be punished as an apostate under the Roman Catholic religion is to be subject to torture and death. Apostasy was the typical charge levied against the victims of the Supreme Sacred Congregation of the Roman and Universal Inquisition during the dark ages. Those who refused to repent of their apostasy were tortured to death. The office of the inquisition still exists today under the title of Sacred Congregation for the Doctrine of the Faith.

    A nun who is confined in a cloistered nunnery can only be interviewed under the most restrictive circumstances. If she is allowed to be interviewed at all, the poor nun is situated behind an impassable metal grating. There is always a third person present, who monitors all that is said to ensure that the nun does not give her honest feelings about her happiness in the cloister.[122]

The restraint of a cloistered nunnery is violative of the most basic principals of freedom and justice. Indeed, the Thirteenth Amendment to the U.S. Constitution prohibits involuntary servitude.

> Neither slavery nor involuntary servitude, except as a punishment for crime whereof the party shall have been duly convicted, shall exist within the United States, or any place subject to their jurisdiction. U.S. Const., 13th Amendment.

To restrain someone from leaving a cloistered nunnery constitutes the crime of false imprisonment. Only the police have the right to detain someone against their will. Under U.S. law the police can only do so if they have probable cause to believe the person detained has committed a crime.[123] An officer can temporarily detain someone for questioning only if the officer has reasonable suspicion that the person has committed or is about to commit a crime.[124]

False imprisonment is both a crime and a civil cause of action. If a person willfully detains another person without their consent and without any justification under the law that person can be prosecuted criminally and sued civilly for false imprisonment.[125]

How is the Catholic Church able to get away with the confinement of nuns against their will in a nunnery? The entire system of cloistered nunneries is based upon the fraud that the nuns have consented to their confinement. A person who consents to confinement may not claim false imprisonment. Certainly, there are nuns who continue to cling to the superstitious Catholic theology and prefer their confinement. However, there is a healthy plurality of nuns who have changed their mind and wish to leave, but are prevented from doing so.

Furthermore, the consent necessary to defeat a claim of false imprisonment must be without duress, coercion, or fraud. That is why cloistered nuns are never allowed to be interviewed without a chaperone (i.e., a spy) to ensure she says that she is happy in the cloister and does not want to leave. A person who is inveigled into a nunnery through tricks and misrepresentations cannot be said to have voluntarily consented to the confinement. When the nun finds that the cloister is not what she has expected and wants to leave, she finds that she is being falsely imprisoned against her will and against the law.

Indeed, most countries have statutes that prohibit the very conduct of the Catholic Church. For example, the U.S. Government has codified Trafficking in Persons statutes. It is a federal felony if a person holds or returns a person to a person to a condition of peonage (18 U.S.C. § 1581); knowingly and willfully holds or sells a person into a condition of involuntary servitude (18 U.S.C. § 1584); kidnaps or carries away a person to be sold into slavery or involuntary servitude (18 U.S.C. § 1583); brings into the United States anyone held in involuntary servitude (18 U.S.C. 1584); entices, persuades, or induces any other person to go on board any vessel or to any other place with the intent that he or she may be made or held as a slave, or sent out of the country to be so made or held (18U.S.C. § 1583); knowingly providing or obtaining the labor or services of a person by means of force, threats of force, physical restraint or threats of physical restraint, serious harm or threats of serious harm, abuse or the threatened abuse of law or legal process, or any scheme or plan that would cause the person to believe that if he did not perform such labor or services that person or another person would suffer serious harm or physical restraint (18 U.S.C. § 1589); knowingly (or in reckless disregard) benefitting, financially or by receiving anything of value, from participation in a venture which has engaged in the providing or obtaining of labor or services by any of the means described above (18 U.S.C. § 1589); knowingly recruiting, harboring, transporting, providing, or obtaining by any means, any person for labor or services under peonage, involuntary servitude, slavery, by means of force or threats of force, by means of serious harm or threats of serious harm (18 U.S.C. § 1590); recruiting, enticing, harboring, transporting, providing, obtaining, or maintaining by any means a person or benefitting, financially or by receiving anything of value, from participation in such conduct while knowing, or in reckless disregard of the fact, that means of force, threats of force, fraud, coercion or any combination of such means will be used to cause the person to engage in a commercial sex act (18 U.S.C. § 1591); recruiting, enticing, harboring, transporting, providing, obtaining, or maintaining by any means a person who has not attained the age of 18 years and will be caused to engage in a commercial sex or benefitting, financially or by receiving anything of value from such a venture (18 U.S.C. § 1591); obstructing or attempting to obstruct or in any way interfering with or preventing the enforcement of 18 U.S.C. §§ 1581, 1584, or 1590.

The penalty for violating sections 1581, 1583, 1584, 1589, and 1590 of Title 18 is a fine or imprisonment of not more than 20 years, or both. If death results from the violation, or if the violation includes kidnapping or an attempt to kidnap, aggravated sexual abuse or the attempt to commit aggravated sexual abuse, or an attempt to kill, the defendant shall be fined or imprisoned for any term of years or life.

The sex trafficking offenses under section 1591 that involve force, threats of force, fraud, or coercion or where a victim who was recruited, enticed, harbored, transported, provided, or obtained had not attained the age of 14 years at the time of such offense, have the punishment of a fine and imprisonment for any term of years not less than 15 years or for life. Where the victim recruited, enticed, harbored, transported, provided, or obtained had attained the age of 14 years but had not attained the age of 18 years at the time of the offense, the punishment would be a fine and imprisonment for not less than 10 years or for life.

There are long-arm provisions in the statutes. Long-arm provisions allow for the enforcement of the statues even though the trafficking in person crime itself is conducted outside the United States. Pursuant to 18 U.S.C. § 1596, any person who commits, attempts to commit or conspires to commit any of the listed trafficking in persons offenses in the United States regardless of their nationality, or any U.S. national or a lawfully admitted alien admitted for U.S. permanent residence who commits any such act anywhere in the world can be prosecuted by the United States for a violation of federal law under the trafficking in persons statutes.

The above statues are based upon common law principles of justice. Many countries, even if they are not common law countries, have similar statutes. How is it that the Catholic Church can confine these women in nunneries even today with such impunity? The answer is found in an episode that took place around 1855, which was recounted by an escaped nun in a book she later wrote. She and another nun escaped from a nunnery; several weeks after their escape they were tricked by a woman to accompany her on a supposed mission of charity for the poor. It was a ruse. Once the two former nuns were enticed away from their protectors, they found themselves kidnaped by the hierarchy of the Catholic Church. The Archbishop of New York held them captive at first in a dungeon and later in a convent. A Protestant lawyer, one Clarence, suspected that they had been kidnaped by the Catholic Church. Clarence was able to win their release from the clutches of the Roman beast. The lawyer's sister explained to one of the nuns later how it was that the Archbishop mysteriously decided to release the nuns.

> [The Protestant lawyer, Clarence,] went directly to the residence of the Archbishop, and informed him of his suspicions respecting your abduction. The Archbishop assumed an air of offended dignity, and angrily denied that he was cognizant of your absence from home; but Clarence was not to be driven from the field. He held up the law as a terror to the high dignitary, but **the Archbishop, with calm effrontery, told him that he held in his grasp the fortunes of those who made the laws, and that they would not dare to attempt an enforcement of any law of the land which was obnoxious to him.** I know not

how it is, but Clarence tells me it is indeed too true, that this proud priest had uttered the truth, and that he felt it in all its potential force; but he tells me that having studied the history of politics for the past few years, and having had occasion to watch the course of this intriguing priest, he knew that there was ONE POWER before which the Archbishop had always quailed, and that power was THE PEOPLE, with their intelligence, their patriotism, and their honesty.

"The People," then exclaimed Clarence, "shall be appealed to; the public square shall be the forum from which I shall speak to the millions; and that portion of the public press which breathes the national spirit, will echo the cry of AN AMERICAN GIRL IN A ROMISH PRISON! until the deafening shouts of a nation's native sons shall shake to earth the prison walls that girdle her about. I go, to invoke the spirit of the people" cried Clarence as he moved towards the door. "Stay, stay!" exclaimed the trembling priest; "you are rash; be not hasty, I will see if your suspicions are well grounded. I promise you, indeed, that no harm shall happen to the girl, if by any chance she has strayed among my people. This is sudden, my dear sir; a little time is needed. I will inquire today at our several houses in the city." [Editor's note: The Archbishop was lying about having to check to find out if the nuns were held captive by the Catholic Church. He knew full well that the nuns were being held captive, as he personally had taken part in their custodial interrogation prior to the arrival of the protestant lawyer at his residence.]

"See that you do then," said Clarence, "and let me know by night, or by the power that made me I will make the city ring with this foul wrong." True to his promise, the cheering word was brought from the Archbishop that you were safe, and that, in a few days, you should be restored to us.[126] (bold emphasis added).

The arrogant Archbishop spoke the truth. The Roman Catholic Church has great political influence. That is how the Roman Church is able to get away with confining women against their will in nunneries because she has political influence, even in a Protestant country like the U.S.

The sad case of Nellie Fortune is one example of the political influence of the Roman Catholic Church in the United States. In an essay on the papacy, Professor David Plaisted quoted from a contemporaneous account of the 1927 escape of Nellie Fortune from a Saint Joseph's Convent in Tipton, Indiana. She was was recaptured by the elected sheriff of Tipton County Indiana and forcibly returned to the convent from which she escaped.

Menace, Feb., 1927

Rome has won another victory, a victory which forever places a dark blot upon the history of one of the strongest Protestant counties in one of the strongest Protestant States in the Union Tipton County, Indiana.

Little Nellie Fortune, a girl of twenty years, Convent Number 096, saw a chance to escape. Although the night was bitter cold she made her way across fields, through woodlands and over streams, finally reaching a farm house a distance of five miles away, before the coming of daylight forced her to seek shelter She crept into an out-building and was found by a kindly farmer and was taken in and given food and clothing. This man was preparing to move and Nellie was taken to the home of a neighbor, Mr. and Mrs. Charlie Fuller of the Rock Prairie community. Here she was welcomed and given a home by this good Protestant family.

She related the many things which take place behind the convent walls of St. Joseph's Convent, and said she could stand the conditions there no longer and resolved to escape or die in the attempt. She had come to America from Northern Ireland, and stated that conditions in the convents here were far worse than they were in Ireland.

She was happy in her new home, telling her

benefactors that "it felt good to be a Protestant." Plans had been made for her to attend church and "be a real Protestant," as she expressed it.

Life was beginning to take on a brighter aspect for poor little Nellie Fortune. She had a good home; she had freedom, and what was more, human love and companionship. But her joy was to be short lived. The unrelenting hounds of Rome were hot on the trail. At last she was located. Sheriff Claud Louks, of Tipton, (elected on a 100 per cent ticket and sworn to defend the American home, etc.) was called and without a warrant or any authority, save the request of the church of Rome, went straightway to the home of Mr. and Mrs. Fuller and seized the pleading, crying, defenseless girl, who begged for her liberty and fought with her last ounce of strength to be permitted to remain with those who had befriended her. Mr. and Mrs. Fuller also pleaded and begged but to no avail.

Nellie was dragged back to the convent of St. Joseph, to face God alone knows what.[127]

Sheriff Claude Louks was born June 10, 1885, in Tipton, Indiana and was a lifelong resident. Louks died of a heart attack on November 10, 1947. His obituary states that he "was a former member of the Kemp Methodist church."[128] Although Louks was a nominal Protestant, he was also a politician. His obituary states: "Active in Democratic politics, Mr. Louks had served as county chairman for the party."[129] There is no doubt that his willingness to serve the interests of the Catholic Church was due to its powerful political influence.

CLAUD LOUKS
Sheriff, 1927

The correct spelling of Louks' first name is "Claude," as that is what appears on his gravestone and in his obituary. Some might find fault with the misspelling of Louks' name as "Claud" in the 1927 narrative. As the caption under the adjacent picture indicates, however, many local people spelled Louks' name, "Claud," without an "e." Indeed, the July 7, 1931, Tipton Tribune spelled Louks' first name as "Claud," when identifying him as "Former Sheriff Claud Louks."[130] Could it be his performance in the Nellie Fortune case was the reason that by 1931 he was no longer sheriff? His obituary indicates that [h]e joined the state police after serving as sheriff."[131] He worked as a lieutenant with the state police for two years. On or about 1927, Louks was elected to a four-year term as sheriff, with 100 percent of the vote. He was the Democratic party chairman in the county. It would seem that he would have been a shoo-in for reelection as sheriff. Yet, four years later, he was out of office and found it necessary to go to work as a lieutenant with the state police. When Louks died 20 years later, he was working as a prison guard at the state reformatory in Pendelton, Indiana. Although Louks may have feared the political influence of the Catholic Church and thought it was a good idea to do their bidding, it seems that the Catholic Church was not of much help to Louks' political career. How ironic that Louks spent his remaining days on earth in a prison working as a guard, after having sent Nellie Fortune to her imprisonment in St. Joseph's Convent. Louks is dead, but the Congregation of Saint Joseph Convent still exists, to this day, in Tipton, Indiana.[132]

Another example of the political influence of the Catholic Church can be found in the case of Olivia Neal, which is recounted by the editor of former nun Josephine Bunkley's book.

> On the 18th of August, 1839, a nun by the name of Olivia Neal, formerly of Charles county, Maryland, but who had been for nineteen years a prisoner, under the appellation of "Sister Isabella," at the Carmelite nunnery in Aisquith Street, Baltimore, succeeded in escaping from that institution. After being repulsed by several families, she was received and protected by a worthy citizen living a few doors from the convent. Efforts were immediately made by the confessor of the convent and others to have access to the fugitive and convey her back. The rumor of this fact having spread in the city, an immense

crowd gathered around the house, and signified their determination to prevent the abduction. The mayor and other gentlemen having come to the spot, she was taken to a place of safety.

This nun stated to all who questioned her that she had entered the convent at a very early age; that she had long desired to escape; that on one occasion before she had gotten out and was met and carried back by the priest. She demanded, in a most earnest and touching manner, the protection of the people.

The assertion was at once made by the authorities of the convent that Olivia Neal, or "Sister Isabella," was out of her right mind. This plea is invariably set up in similar cases. A physician was induced to state that she was a "perfect maniac;" and five others united in the conflicting statement that she was a "monomaniac" or at least afflicted with a "general feebleness of intellect." Hundreds, however, of the most respectable citizens of Baltimore concurred in declaring that Miss Neal gave every indication of sanity, correct judgment, and resolute will.

The Reverend Robert J. Breckinridge, D.D., a distinguished and most estimable clergyman of the Presbyterian Church, was at that time a resident of Baltimore, and was requested to have an interview with this escaped nun. He thus relates it: "As we entered the room, he [a friend] said to her, 'This is Mr. B.,' naming us. "Her reply went to our heart. She extended her hands toward us, and, repeating our name, said, almost convulsively, 'I claim your protection!' We told her we had come to her for no other purpose.

"A rapid conversation, in which several took part, immediately ensued, from which we learned, in substance, that her name was Olivia Neal, originally from Charles county, Maryland, but now called 'Sister Isabella;' that she had been put into the convent very young, and been in it nineteen years; that she had been long anxiously trying to get out, and had once succeeded in making her escape into the street, when she was met and forcibly carried back, and subjected to severe penances; that, having again escaped, her anxious desire was for present protection a desire she repeatedly expressed; that, however, she wished all to understand that she did not desire to change her religion, but only her condition as a nun; that she did not wish any violence offered either to the nuns or priests on her account, against whom, indeed, she was not disposed to make any accusations; that she felt agitated, and unfit for any extended conversation on the subject of her past trials, and asked only for security, repose, and tranquillity, till she could collect her faculties and decide on her future line of conduct, which was the more necessary, she said, as they had told her that her mind was weak ; and that, having no friends in whom she could confide, she was obliged to throw herself on the public for protection.

"Much more was said, which we do not think it worth while to repeat at present; but, as a sample of the general style of conversation, we will detail one item more minutely. She was asked if a nun had not escaped some months ago. 'Yes; it was I,' was her reply. 'How happens it that you were back again?' 'I was met by a gentleman immediately after getting out, and carried back.' 'Who was that gentleman?' No answer. 'Was it priest Gildea?' 'Yes, sir.' 'What was done to you when you were carried back?' 'There are penances to undergo; I was subjected to these.' 'Did they whip you?' No answer, but a mournful smile. 'Did they imprison you ?' 'I have said I endured the usual penance.' She was not pressed farther on this painful subject, being evidently unwilling to speak fully of it."[133]

The sequel to this sad story of oppression and suffering exhibits the triumph of Romish intrigue over the natural and legal rights of a feeble woman. A distant relative was found who was willing to serve the purposes of priestly craft. He came to Baltimore, obtained ex parte certificates contradictory of each other, insufficient in law or reason, none of which were sworn to, and no cross examination permitted; on which certificates he took his kinswoman and placed her precisely where she had most earnestly desired never to go again under the power of the nuns and priests. Nothing more has been heard of her for years. Miss Bunkley, in the preceding narrative, mentions having seen in the asylum at Mount Hope a person who, as she had reason to believe, was the unhappy "Sister Isabella."[134]

The fate of 'Sister Isabella' is the fate of all citizens who exchange their God-given rights of life, liberty, and property for the group privileges bestowed upon them by the government. The Catholic religion is inherently collectivist and communal along the Marxist line. Under Roman Catholicism rights are not individual, God-given rights, as in the Christian gospel. Rather, they are collective group privileges that flow from government under the Talmudic philosophy of communism. For a more detailed review of the evidence of Catholic communism, read this author's book, *Solving the Mystery of Babylon the Great*. Indeed, Sister Jesme in her 2009 book, *The Autobiography of a Nun*, stated: "'From each according to their capacity and to each according to their need' is the norm practiced in the congregation."[135] That statement is a paraphrase of the major plank of Marxist Communism. Sister Jesme further stated: "The late Bishop

Mankuzhikary once told the public: 'You want to meet the real Marxists. Look here.'"[136] It is the objective of the Roman Catholic church to transform this nation's government from a respecter of individual rights to a socialist grantor of government privileges. The Roman beast desires to take hold of the reigns of government and crush the individual rights of its citizens.

15 An Authoritative Exposè of Nunneries

Dear reader we have the privilege of reading the authoritative opinion of a high official of the Roman Church. Dr. Luigi de Sanctis, as a Catholic priest was the "qualificator" of the Office of the Inquisition. In that capacity, he was relied upon by the prelates of Rome as the authority on issues of Catholic theology. He was saved by the grace of God out of his Roman error to the glorious grace of God in the true gospel of Jesus Christ. The following is an extract from a letter that Dr. de Sanctis sent to the publishers of Josephine Bunkley's 1855 book, *The Testimony of an Escaped Novice*.[137]

> We have now to present some extracts from a letter addressed to the editor of this work by the distinguished and excellent Dr. De Sanctis, who occupied for many years the post of curate of the church of the Maddalena at Rome, was "qualificator" of the Inquisition, censor of the Theological

Academy in the Roman University, and filled other prominent offices of trust in the service of the Church of Rome. He was in this capacity commissioned by the Cardinal Vicar to preach and hear confessions in the convents of that city; and during ten years and more, passed scarcely a day in which he did not exercise these functions at some one or more of those institutions. Written by one so competent to speak from personal observation upon the subject of monasticism, and so worthy of trust as an able and faithful minister of the Gospel since his conversion from Roman Catholic error, we are sure that these statements will command the attention of our readers.

THE CONVENT A PRISON OF DELUSIONS.

"The convents of Rome may be designated as prisons—horrible prisons of religious delusion. This statement will require some explanation. A young girl at Rome, who is to any degree interested in religion, if she receives her education at a convent, must absolutely remain there forever, as I shall hereafter explain; or, if not so educated, must necessarily enter a convent in the end. The Roman Catholic priest knows nothing of conjugal love in its holy and chaste character, and for this very reason he hates it, he detests it, often with the utmost sincerity and perfect good faith. The declamations of the priests, whether from the pulpit or the confessional, against this love, are of a nature to make one shudder. These men are truly to be pitied: ignorant as they are of the pure, the legitimate affection of the married state, and knowing only of a sensual and bestial passion, they have reason to declaim against such love. The young girl who blindly follows the path of piety, blindly believes the priest; for want of experience, she can not distinguish the innocent from the guilty affection; and when she feels the first impulses of that love which would lead her to become a wife and a mother, she confesses to the priest as a grave offense those sentiments which pertain to the normal state in which God has framed her being. And the confessor, most generally from ignorance, and with honest persuasion, augments this uneasiness, declaring that this impulse is a temptation of the devil in order to eradicate the love of Christ. He intimates that there is no better method of overcoming such temptation than to fly from a world which is but a troubled sea, and to withdraw into the haven of security, to wit, the convent. And here he commences to adduce before the kindled imagination of his charge all those mystic incidents, examples, histories, and revelations, of which the legendary literature of asceticism is full, thus inflaming the mind of the young penitent, and convincing her that there is no harbor of safety for her soul other than the state of a recluse. All that she sees in the world without becomes to her an object of aversion. The persons most endeared by natural affection father, mother, brothers become odious, and she longs for the moment when she may inclose herself within those sacred walls, where alone she now hopes to find peace and salvation. The world is represented to her as a wild and corrupt stream, flowing with impetuous current before her, while the convent, overlooking it, offers the only secure retreat. Her father, her brother, her sisters are being carried away by the river; for her there is safety only there. The dream lasts a while after she has entered, and then it disappears; the abode of peace is transformed into a perpetual prison, where a life pays for the religious delusion of a day.

"Many young girls are drawn to the convents in this manner, but there are others, and perhaps these constitute a majority, who are attracted in a different way. Many, to whom nature has denied those external graces and charms which captivate the regard of men, finding themselves neglected, and conscious of an irresistible need of loving some object, seek to be loved, as they say, by our Lord Jesus Christ. 'The heart of Jesus' is the chosen devotion of such. It is after this fashion that the 'heart of Jesus' is represented at Rome. Our Lord is depicted as a young man of marvelous beauty, who, with a heart shining with love, seen transparent in his breast, invites with the most winning look. The young girl who has not met with a response in the regard of men, enthusiastically begins to cherish an affection for this picture and object. The priests know well how to encourage such a tendency; they place in her hands the lives of St. Teresa and other visionaries, who relate their intercourse with a heavenly spouse, and already she hopes that a like experience will be hers. Another need that she feels is that of making some human heart the depository of her thoughts and emotions, and for want of a lover she chooses as a confidant her confessor. With him she spends whole hours of every day in secret colloquies, and, supposing the confessor to be a saint, according to the Romish idea, the unavoidable result of all this is that she will go into a convent. The dream after a while is scattered, and there remains the sad reality of a perpetual prison as the fruit of a religious delusion.

"There is a third class of young persons, who, being educated from childhood in the nunnery, remain there, and become nuns without knowing why, and give up with alacrity a world which they have never seen. By what arts and wiles they are drawn into this course I shall relate elsewhere, when I come to speak of the education given in convents.

MORALITY OP THE CONVENTS IN ROME.

"Such is, for the most part, the method by which the convents of Rome are peopled. I must now say a few words respecting the morality of those institutions.

"That there have occurred some flagrant abuses of this nature, and more especially in convents where the education of the young is prosecuted, can not be denied. Two fearful examples have taken place within my own recollection, the general publicity of which created a painful excitement. The one occurred at the Convent of '*San Dionisio alle quattro Fontane*,' an establishment of nuns affiliated with the Jesuits, in which the confessor pursued a most infamous course in relation to a large number of young persons under the care of that institution. The other case was that of the '*Conservatorio della Divina Providenza*,' where the confessor seduced no fewer than sixteen of the most beautiful persons educated in that convent. * * * * As a general thing, however, the convent (so far as Rome is concerned) is neither, on the one hand, a terrestrial paradise inhabited by angels, nor, on the other hand, is it generally a place of open and shameless crime.

"An event of no unfrequent occurrence in the convent is the 'spiritual assistance' of the sick. When a nun is dangerously ill, the confessor, director, or another priest spends the night at the institution. Often it will happen that, in a case of sickness, fifteen or sixteen successive nights are thus spent. This has happened more than once to myself. In the convent there are generally two well-furnished rooms for such a contingency: the one is a small parlor, conveniently arranged, where the confessor eats; the other a bedroom, where, also, nothing is omitted for his comfort. The supper of the reverend father confessor is no ordinary one; it consists of all the niceties of food that are to be procured. While the holy man is at his meal, several nuns will be standing around him, urging him to eat this and drink that. Supper over, the father goes to see the patient, sprinkles her with holy water, and then retires to his bed. The doors are left open, in order that he may readily be called should the invalid grow worse. 'I cannot say that all precautions are taken in such cases, nor that disorders fail to occur, and that with sufficient frequency. I can only state matters as I know them to exist.

"And here I may incidentally mention a fact that will surprise the good Christian people of America, although at Rome it appears quite natural. In Carnival, (a period of five or six days preceding Lent, during which, in Roman Catholic countries, every species of merriment and buffoonery is tolerated) the inmates of all the convents are permitted the masquerade. The monks who act as confessors send their habits to their respective nuns, who put them on, and enact a thousand ridiculous scenes. Any one can understand the indecency, and, to speak more clearly, the immorality of such procedures; but this is nothing: on the contrary, it seems so natural that a nun who should fail to join in these amusements would be regarded as over-scrupulous even by her confessor himself. In convents devoted to education, there are, besides these, theatrical performances, and comedies are recited. To these representations are admitted the confessors, priests, monks, and the relatives of the nuns and pupils. On such occasions you would see some one of these young girls ornamented with mustaches, declaiming the part of an officer, and dressed in uniform, while another would take the character of a lover, etc., etc. In convents where superior sanctity is affected, profanations still greater are committed. There are given dramatic entertainments called sacred, and these are nothing less than Scripture facts set forth in comedy. There you would see a young girl assuming the part of Moses, another that of Aaron, thus turning into ridicule those holy characters, and casting contempt upon the word of God itself. I once saw at one of these places a young person who represented an angel, while another filled the role of the devil. Between them they concocted a dialogue so ludicrous that every body was exploding with laughter.

HEALTH IN THE CONVENTS OF ROME.

"In order to make what I have to say respecting these institutions more clear, let me divide them into two classes: the one consisting of those where the inmates have no other occupation besides prayer, the other in which they are employed in giving instruction to the young.

With regard to the former class, we must again distinguish those convents where the rigor of discipline is carried to such an excess of fanaticism as to tread under foot the most sacred laws of nature; and here I do not speak of individual excesses of fanaticism, but of abuses belonging to the community itself, approved and sanctioned by the Superiors of the institution.

There is at Rome, in the *'Regione de'*

Monti,' in a spot almost unknown to the world, a convent entitled that of the '*Vive Sepolte*' ('buried alive') (More properly, *Religiose Fruncescane dette 'Vive Sepolte*'); and the miserable inmates are really in the condition expressed by their name. Once admitted within those walls, it may be said of them,

'Leave hope behind, all ye who enter here.'

"They are indeed buried alive. They come to confession, but a double grating, the one at a considerable distance from the other, an iron plate punctured with small holes between the confessor and the penitent, through which the voice can scarcely pass, and a black cloth fastened upon this plate to intercept even the rays of light such is the mode in which the confession takes place. When these nuns commune, they present themselves at a small window, about half the size of the countenance; and there, with a thick woolen cloth over the face, suffering only the tongue to be seen, they receive the element from the hand of the priest. In case of sickness, they are led into a room called the infirmary, and there the physician prescribes for his patient through an aperture in the wall. If he wishes to feel the pulse or draw blood, the arm of the invalid must be extended to him through the aperture.

"The physician of this convent related to me these facts as I was visiting the institution, and stated that many of the nuns had died in consequence of these impediments to a proper medical attendance. He told me that on one occasion, indignant at this suicidal course, he went to Cardinal Patrizi, the patron of this convent, who replied to his complaint that there was no need of interference, these persons being, not suicides, but victims of holy modesty.

"When the nun enters this establishment, she is, I have said, 'buried alive.' She must henceforth know nothing of her relatives. Once in the year it is allowed that relatives of the first degree present themselves at the monastery, and speak in the hearing of the recluse; they may not, however, see the countenance of their daughter or sister. When a near relative of a nun dies, the Mother Superior, on the evening after that event, says at prayers, 'My sisters, let us pray for the soul of the father, or mother, or brother of one of our number, who died yesterday or today;' and it is not permitted that any one know who it is that has died: hence each imagines that it may be her own father, mother, or brother; and in this uncertainty she is left, in order that she may, with more fervor, from day to day, pray for the deceased. Such is the abuse that fanaticism makes of religion! But things of this sort are not generally known or believed, and for this reason I state and affirm the facts. If you should publish them, do so with my name, as I am willing to be responsible for them.

"When a youth, I resided in the neighborhood of this convent, and I remember that one day the Pope, Leo XII., made an unexpected visit to the institution. It excited much curiosity in the quarter to know the occasion of this visit, which was as follows: A woman had an only daughter who had taken the veil in that convent. Left a widow, she came often to the institution, and with a mother's tears besought that she might be allowed, if not to see, at least to hear the voice of her daughter. "What request more just and more sacred from a mother? But what is there of sacredness and justice that fanaticism does not corrupt? The daughter sent word by the confessor to her mother that if she did not cease to importune her, she would refuse to speak to her even on the day when she would be allowed to do so. That day at length arrived; the widowed mother was the first to present herself at the door of the convent, and she was told that she could not see her daughter. In despair, she asked Why? No answer. Was she sick? No reply. Was she dead? Not a word. The miserable mother conjectured that her daughter was dead. She ran to the Superiors to obtain at least the privilege of seeing her corpse, but their hearts were of iron. She went to the Pope: a mother's tears touched the breast of Leo XII., and he promised her that on the following morning he would be at the convent and ascertain the fact. He did so, as I have said, unexpectedly to all. Those doors, which were accustomed to open only for the admittance of a fresh victim, opened that day to the head of the Church of Rome. Seeing the wretched mother who was the occasion of this visit, he called her to him, and ordered her to follow him into the nunnery. The daughter, who, by an excess of barbarous fanaticism, thought to please Heaven by a violation of the holiest laws of nature, concealed herself upon hearing that her mother had entered the convent. The Pope called together in a hall the entire sisterhood, and commanded them to lift the veils from their faces. The mother's heart throbbed with vehemence; she looked anxiously from face to face once and again, but her daughter was not there. She believed now that she was dead, and, with a piercing cry, fell down in a swoon. While she was reviving, the Pope peremptorily asked the Mother Superior whether the daughter was dead or alive. She replied, at length, that she was yet living, but having vowed to God that she would eradicate every carnal affection from her breast, she was unwilling even to see her mother again. It was not until the Pope ordered her appearance, in virtue of the obedience due to him, and upon pain of mortal sin, that the nun came forth. This outrage upon human nature, which might have resulted in parricide, is denominated in the vocabulary of monasticism '*virtue in heroic degree.*'

"Besides the convent of the '*Vive Sepolte*,' there are at Rome other institutions of a similar cast; for example, that of the Capuchin nuns of San Urbano, those of Monte Cavallo, the Teresians of San Giuseppe a Capo le case, those of San Eligio in Trastevere, and so forth. Numbers of these poor wretches every year commit suicide through a false spirit of penitence. They go without necessary food; they wear haircloth when nature demands restoratives; they refuse themselves remedies which would arrest disease, and this from a false modesty which forbids the communicating of their ailments to the physician. Many have I known to die of such procedure. You will call these nuns poor victims of delusion ; the world will call them mad; but, in the dictionary of the convent, they are termed '*holy martyrs of sacred modesty.*'

"I will not relate to you all the minutiae of the convent life; it would take a volume instead of a letter to do so. Imagine what must be an establishment where fifty or sixty women live, as it were, in a prison women brought together without knowledge of one another, gnawing the curb of an imprisonment which they affect to make appear voluntary, and which they seek to persuade themselves is such and you will perceive what must be the nature of their life. * * * * Suicide by means of the rope or poison is not a very frequent occurrence in nunneries at Rome, but a species of suicide little known to the world is most frequent there: I mean that which proceeds from imprudent penances, the injurious repression of innocent affections, the persistent effort to contradict and thwart nature in every possible mode, the refusal, from false modesty, to make known, for medical advice, whatever maladies may occur these and other reasons suffice to account for the fact that a very considerable proportion of nuns perish in youth, and so many others drag through years an existence of continued ailments and infirmities. * * *

THE NUNS AND THEIR CONFESSORS.

"There are other convents of 'contemplative life;' such is the appellation given to those where the principal occupation is or ought to be prayer in which matters proceed quite differently from the '*Vive Sepolte*.' At such institutions you would see, from early in the morning till evening, a string of priests and monks going and coming; these are the confessors of the nuns. To enable you to understand this more clearly, let me say that for each convent there is a confessor, so called. This confessor is a priest, appointed by the bishop and supported by the nunnery, who must always be at the convent for the 'spiritual direction' of its inmates. He is the pastor of the community, and all ought, according to rule, to confess to him. But it is not the practice of nuns to confess to the ordinary confessor. Each one has her own in particular, and some have two or three; but these particular confessors can not be called by that name; they are termed ' directors.' Each ' director,' as he reaches the institution, is received by his nun, who, if it be in the morning, regales him with a cup of excellent chocolate, or, after dinner, with refreshments, of which sweetmeats always form a part. While this holy director is eating, his nun converses with him; ordinarily the interview lasts about half an hour; then they go and shut themselves up in a confessional, where they remain at least an hour. This occurs at least twice a week, and often every day. The conversation is commonly any thing but religious; it is apt to consist chiefly of small-talk and scandal. * * *

"I have promised to speak of those convents which are devoted to education and instruction. Nearly all the nunneries contain some young persons who are in process of education, and are supported there by their relatives for this purpose; but there are convents which have for their principal scope the instruction of youth. For these institutions the description I have given of the others will, in general, answer to the truth; but it must be added that the young persons receiving their education at the convent do not know all that takes place in the establishment. They live in a particular portion of it, separate from the greater part of the nuns, whom they see only in the choir and at the refectory. They are under the charge of a nun who superintends their education.

"But wherein does this education consist? Culture of intellect they can not derive from the reading of ascetic books, legendaries, lives of the saints, and particularly from those works which speak of the felicities of the monastic life and the horrors of the world. In their tender minds this is the cardinal idea inculcated, that outside of the cloister it is almost impossible to find salvation. All books save those that speak of these things are absolutely prohibited. Hence geography, history, and all other branches of useful and necessary knowledge are completely banished from these places as worldly studies.

"The culture of the heart is shockingly profaned. Ignoring the life of the family, they learn to detest it. With the pretext that every human relation is profane, they alienate themselves, under the garb of sanctity, from parental love. They love none but those whom they believe to stand in the place of God the confessor foremost of all, and then the mother mistress. Should one of these young persons leave the convent and marry (I relate what I have known in many cases), broils and strifes arise in the domestic circle. She refuses to obey her husband until the confessor has instructed her in matrimonial duties, and has commanded her to obey. Is this always innocence? I answer, No.

"For a young girl educated in a convent to be a good wife and a good mother is a thing most rare. At Rome it is a common saying, 'Do you want a faithless woman? Marry a girl brought up at a nunnery.' This rule has its exceptions, but be assured they are exceptions; fifteen years of experience at the confessional have taught me this. Such a person can not be a good mother, because, not educated in the family, she knows nothing of domestic life. She can not be a good housekeeper, because the superintendence of a household is something to her quite new. Few are the husbands who have not speedy cause to repent of marrying a young girl just out of the convent. With regard to work, the nuns teach only how to embroider church cloths.

"There is some difference, however, in the case of those convents which are destined more particularly for the education of the young. Of this nature there are at Rome the nunnery of '*Torre di Specchi*,' for the high aristocracy; that of the ' Sacred Heart,' embracing all classes of persons; and that of the ' Ursulines,' for the middle class. * * * At the ' Sacred Heart,' the instruction given is certainly better than at other convents; but let us examine its character. Geography is taught; it may, however, be denominated geography applied to Jesuitism. Respecting every country and kingdom described, it is explained whether there be Jesuits in it, how much good they have done if there, how much evil has resulted if they have been driven away. History is taught; with the sole design, however, of convincing that Popery and Jesuitism are the only source of all good, and that where these have not been found, every crime and horror has thriven. Thus the young mind is so thoroughly imbued with prejudice, that it shudders at the bare mention of Henry the Eighth, Cromwell, or Washington. * * * The religious instruction consists of weak superstitions. She who can best adorn the image of her favorite saint, whom she changes every month, is the most devout.

NATURAL AFFECTIONS DESTROYED.

"That, however, which constitutes the chief object of instruction, and wherein the nuns wonderfully succeed, is the eradication of filial love and respect, to be supplanted by a blind obedience to the priests. And thus it is that they proceed. Two principal motives are brought into play for this purpose—pride and religion. They begin by exalting the freedom of the individual. They say that it is a gift of God, and we must not suffer it to be taken away. A doctrine most true; but listen to the application. The parents of the young girl propose to her, for instance, a match, it may be most desirable. The young girl has been taught to look upon this proposal as an attempt upon her individual liberty, and she accordingly declines. Her parents endeavor to persuade her ; they urge that they do not wish to compel her assent, but only recommend what seems for the best. She, however, has learned from the nuns a quantity of stories about young people who have been rendered miserable by acceding to the will of their parents, and she persists in her refusal. The parents then are obliged to go to the confessor, and obtain of him that he will persuade the young girl. The confessor gathers information respecting the person in question, and if the match suit the Jesuits, the young girl will be persuaded, otherwise her disinclination will increase. Say what you will of the father and mother being her best friends, the most deserving of confidence—domestic life has become extinguished in the convent; for its inmate there is no father but the confessor, no mother but the 'mistress mother.'

"But, beside this motive of self-will, that of religion is brought in to set aside the parental right. This seems incredible; it is nevertheless a fact. The favorite principle that constitutes the theme of the exhortations of the 'mistress mother' is the explanation I should say, rather, the infamous perversion, of a passage in the Gospel, 'He that loveth father or mother more than me, is not worthy of me.' From this text they inculcate upon these youthful minds that when they feel themselves inspired to do or not to do any thing, they are not to listen to their parents, who may command or counsel them against that inspiration, otherwise they would love father or mother more than Jesus Christ, and render themselves unworthy of him. Then, to assure themselves of such inspiration, there is but one method—to consult the confessor. The confessor, being consulted, replies that first of all it is requisite to spend some time in prayer; he therefore prescribes a *'novena'* [nine days' devotion] to the 'Sacred Heart,' or to some favorite saint; mean while he ascertains the facts of the case. If the result of this inquiry be favorable, and the young girl feels herself inspired to say *No*, then he shows her that the inspiration is a temptation which must be withstood. If his decision be negative, then the opinion of the confessor, harmonizing with the *no* of the young girl, proves it to be a real inspiration from God. The whole family may go to ruin, it matters not, because 'he that loveth father or mother more than me, is not worthy of me.'

"With such principles as these, a young person educated at a convent becomes a blind instrument in the hands of the Jesuits. Imagine how good a daughter, wife, and mother she will prove.

"I have thus given you, dear sir, a rapid sketch of the nunneries of Rome. I can assure you that I have stated only what I have seen and known from close observation, to the truth of which I pledge myself. Believe me your devoted servant and brother in Jesus Christ,

"L. DE SANCTIS, D.D.,

"Minister of the Holy Gospel.

"LONDON, Sept. 20th, 1855."[138]

16 Unusual Corroboration

William Stone inadvertently confirmed Maria Monk's story. Stone reveals the following, which at the time he probably thought was an insignificant detail. Stone explained: "Soon after we commenced our investigations, we were presented to the lady superior, at the door of her apartment, into which we were admitted. She was suffering from an attack of rheumatism. She is a lady of dignity and refinement of manner; somewhat advanced in years. She received us with the utmost urbanity, nay, with cordiality; and regretted not being able to accompany us through the institution."[139]

Stone had not read Maria Monk's book in its entirety and therefore did not know that he had inadvertently confirmed the description of the lady superior given by Maria Monk in her book. Maria Monk described the lady superior as suffering from swelled limbs that gave her great distress.

THE OLD MOTHER SU-
PERIOR.

While in the nunnery, it was suddenly announced to Maria and the other nuns that the old superior was no longer there, being replaced, without explanation, by a new superior. "The lady he introduced to us was one of our oldest nuns, Saint Du ****, a very large, fleshy woman, with swelled limbs, which rendered her very slow in walking, and often gave her great distress."[140] She was the lady superior in residence when Maria Monk escaped from the cloistered nunnery. Maria's description matches precisely Stone's description of the lady superior. Indeed, she was so suffering when Stone arrived that she could not accompany them on their tour of the nunnery. Maria Monk documented the arthritic lady superior in her book before Stone visited the nunnery. The only way that Maria Monk could have known the condition of the lady superior of the Hotel Dieu Nunnery would be if she herself had been a nun in the convent and had seen her painful condition.

THE NEW MOTHER SUPERIOR.

Furthermore, Maria Monk gave the specific names and physical descriptions of over one hundred priests whose parishes were scattered all over Canada. The only way in which Maria Monk could have possibly known that information was if she had personally seen those priests. That indicates that the priests were seen by her during their visits to the Hotel Dieu Nunnery when present there for sexual interludes with the nuns. As confirmation of these facts, she listed the names of the priests in the appendix to her later edition of her book. The significance of her descriptions of the priests is explained in the appendix.

> It is readily admitted, that any person could take one of the Ecclesiastical Registers of Lower Canada, and at his option mark any number of the Roman Priests in the catalogue, and impute to them any crime which he pleased. But if the accuser were closely examined, and among such a multitude of Priests, who in all their clothing are dressed alike, were called upon minutely to delineate them, it is morally impossible, that he could depict more than a hundred Priests dispersed from the borders of Upper Canada to Quebec, in as many different parishes, with the most perfect accuracy, unless he was personally and well acquainted with them.
>
> Maria Monk, however, does most accurately describe all the Priests in the preceding catalogue, and repeats them at the expiration of weeks and months; and the question is this: how is it possible that

she could have become acquainted with so many of that body, and by what means can she so precisely depict their external appearance?—The startling, but the only plausible answer which can be given to that question is this: that she has seen them in the Nunnery, whither, as she maintains, most of them constantly resorted for licentious intercourse with the Nuns.

One other connected fact may here be introduced. Maria Monk well knows the Lady Superior of the Charlestown Nunnery. That acquaintance could not have been made in the United States, because Saint Mary St. George as she called herself, or Sarah Burroughs, daughter of the notorious Stephen Burroughs, as is her real name, removed to Canada at the latter end of May, 1835; nor could it have been prior to the establishment of the Charlestown Nunnery, for at that period Maria Monk was a child, and was not in any Convent except merely as a scholar; and Mary St. George was at Quebec. How then did she become so familiar with that far-famed lady as to be able to describe her so exactly? The only answer is, that she derived her knowledge of the Charlestown Convent and of its Superior, from the intimations given, and from intercourse with that Nun in the Hotel Dieu Nunnery.[141]

17 Nun's Island

Furthermore, Maria Monk explained in detail her experience on Nun's Island, which is a Catholic monastic enclave on an Island in the Saint Lawrence River. Maria gave an account of how she was used as an unwitting accomplice in the poisoning of a priest by another priest, Patrick Phelan on Nun's Island.[142] Only those authorized by the mother superior, the rector of the seminary, or the bishop are allowed on the secretive Nun's Island. The Catholic hierarchy has by its silence loudly confirmed the authenticity of Maria Monk's account. Maria Monk was able to give a detailed description of the exterior and interior of the buildings, all of which are blocked from public view by a high wall surrounding the complex of buildings, which are situated on a secluded island. There is no way that Maria Monk would know the details of the layout of the complex of buildings unless she had been there. There has been no attempt to refute Maria's account of her stay on Nun's Island or detailed description of the layout of the buildings.

18 Physical Proof

Final and irrefutable corroboration is found in an account that Maria Monk gave of an episode where she was abused in the Hotel Dieu Nunnery. The significance of the account is that it establishes facts that indisputably confirm that she was a nun at the Hotel Dieu Nunnery.

> The Superior ordered me to the cells, and a scene of violence commenced which I will not attempt to describe, nor the precise circumstances which led to it. Suffice it to say, that after exhausting my strength, by resisting as long as I could against several nuns, I had my hands drawn behind my back, a leathern band passed first round my thumbs, then round my hands, and then round my waist, and fastened. **This was drawn so tight that it cut through the flesh of my thumbs, making wounds, the scars of which still remain.** A gag was

then forced into my mouth, not indeed so violently as it sometimes was, but roughly enough; after which I was taken by main force, and carried down into the cellar, across it almost to the opposite extremity, and brought to the last of the second range of cells on the left hand. The door was opened, and I was thrown in with violence, and left alone, the door being immediately closed and bolted on the outside. The bare ground was under me, cold and hard as if it had been beaten down even. I lay still, in the position in which I had fallen, as it would have been difficult for me to move, confined as I was, and exhausted by my exertions; and the shock of my fall, and my wretched state of desperation and fear, disinclined me from any further attempt. I was in almost total darkness, there being nothing perceptible except a slight glimmer of light which came in through the little window far above me. How long I remained in that condition I can only conjecture. It seemed to me a long time, and must have been two or three hours. I did not move, expecting to die there, and in a state of distress which I cannot describe, from the tight bandage about my hands, and the gag holding my jaws apart at their greatest extension. I am confident I must have died before morning, if, as I then expected, I had been left there all night.

After a time, Maria was finally released from her

bonds by the mother superior. Maria Monk explained the wounds that such abuse left on her body.

> Among the marks which I still bear of the wounds received from penances and violence, are the scars left by the belt with which I repeatedly tortured myself, for the mortification of my spirit. These are most distinct on my side; for although the band, which was four or five inches in breadth, and extended round the waist, was stuck full of sharp iron points in all parts, it was sometimes crowded most against my side, by rocking in my chair, and the wounds were usually deeper there than anywhere else. My thumbs were several times cut severely by the tight drawing of the band used to confine my arms, and the scars are still visible upon them. The rough gagging which I several times endured wounded my lips very much; for it was common, in that operation, to thrust the gag hard against the teeth, and catch one or both the lips, which were sometimes cut. The object was to stop the screams made by the offender as soon as possible; and some of the old nuns delighted in tormenting us. A gag was once forced into my mouth which had a large splinter upon it, and this cut through my under lip, in front, leaving to this day a scar about half an inch long. The same lip was several times

> wounded, as well as the other; but one day worse than ever, when a narrow piece was cut off from the left side of it, by being pinched between the gag and the under fore-teeth; and this has left an inequality in it which is still very observable.[143]

In Maria Monk's narrative we have the very evidence to either confirm or refute her allegations. If she was never in the nunnery, as the Catholic church alleges, she would not bear on her body the marks of the abuse she alleges. If the scars are present on her body, their imprint act as the seal of proof upon her allegations.

Were those scars on her body? The answer is yes. Minister J.J. Slocum stated that a respectable lady inspected Maria Monk for signs of scars from the leather belt lined with sharp points of which Maria spoke. The lady confirmed that Maria's body bore clearly evident scars of the pointed belt. The lady stated that "it looks distressing."[144] Further, Slocum could see for himself that "[t]he marks of gagging are seen on her lips; and there are scars also on her thumbs, which were 'cut severely by the tight drawing of the band used to confine her arms.'"[145]

Here we have on Maria's body the very imprint of truth that confirms her account of the abuse in the Hotel Dieu Nunnery. There is simply no other way to account the strange scaring manifest on Maria Monk's body other than according to Maria Monk's explanation. Those scars stood as silent witnesses corroborating the truth of Maria Monk's report.

19 A Nun Corroborates Maria Monk

Within a year of Maria Monk's escape, another nun escaped from the Hotel Dieu Nunnery. Her name was Sainte Frances Patrick (a/k/a Frances Partridge). She corroborated Maria Monk's account of torture, rape, and infanticide at the Hotel Dieu Nunnery. Of course, the Roman Catholic Church responded to Miss Partridge's allegations by stating that she was an impostor.

Samuel B. Smith, who was a former Catholic priest, interviewed Miss Partridge. Mr. Smith was not just any former Catholic priest. He was a former superintendent of a nunnery. The Roman Catholic Church has never disputed Mr. Smith's authenticity as a former Catholic priest and superintendent of a nunnery.

Mr. Smith was well acquainted with the inner-workings of convents; as the superintendent, he was the confessor for the resident nuns, who revealed to him the many secrets of the convent. Mr. Smith was someone who could not be easily deceived by an impostor nun. He determined that Miss Partridge to was an authentic escaped nun from the Hotel Dieu Nunnery in Montreal, and that she was telling the truth.

We are not left only with Mr. Smith's bare opinion regarding the credibility of Miss Partridge. Mr. Smith set forth some objective facts that form the foundation of his assessment of Miss Partridge. Mr. Smith stated that Miss Partridge's manners were of the distinct nature "of those who have been excluded from the world in the solitude of the cloister, particularly characteristic; and which entirely precludes the possibility of being counterfeited."[146]

As with Maria Monk, Miss Partridge bore on her body the marks of the torture that she underwent inside the nunnery. For example, Miss Partridge's face bore the scars of the gag, which Maria Monk described being used in the nunnery. Miss Partridge's face also bore scars that were caused by an instrument that Mr. Smith described as the *Penance of Pins*. The wounds, which had entirely healed, were caused by pins used as a penance that punctured the cheek through to the interior of the mouth. The scars could clearly be seen on both of Miss Partridges cheeks, near her mouth.

Miss Partridge also had an unusual marking of four little dots on her left hand, resembling the dots on dice. They were deeply set in the skin and black in color. Mr. Smith's description suggests that it was some type of tattoo. Mr. Smith explained that those types of marks were given by priests to nuns as a designation that the nun belonged exclusively to that particular priest. Mr. Smith revealed that some nuns receive no mark.

The most startling confirmation of the authenticity of Miss Partridge as an escaped nun comes from the Roman Church itself. In Maria Monk's book, she mentioned an old nun who taught her in school when she was a teenager, before Maria became a nun. The nun's name was "Saint Patrick," who was described by Maria as being at the time about forty years old, with facial hair, ignorant, and disagreeable in her manners.[147] This was not the "Sainte Frances Patrick" described above who met with Mr. Smith, but another nun.

The Roman hierarchy, knowing that Maria Monk had described a "Saint Patrick" nun with some specificity in her book, decided to deceive the uniformed reader by comparing her description with a different Saint Patrick, thus claiming that Maria Monk was wrong in her description. The Jesuits performed this dissembling in a book, in which there is no author attributed, titled, *Awful Exposure of the Atrocious Plot Formed by Certain Individuals Against the Clergy and Nuns of Lower Canada Through the Intervention of Maria Monk*. In the book, the Jesuits attempted to argue that Maria Monk was not to be believed because the "Saint Patrick" to which she referred in her book was not 40 years old with a beard but rather 27 years old without any signs of a beard. The Jesuits stated:

> It is stated at page 30, that among the nuns of the Congregation there is a certain Saint Patrick, "an old woman for a nun" (that is, about forty) with quite a beard." The only truth in this is, that Saint Patrick is the Conventual name of one of the sisterhood; the talent of the witness has expanded it into a falsehood. Saint Patrick is now

(1836) in her twenty-seventh year; and unfortunately for the description, has as yet betrayed no appearance of a "beard."

As we have no means of ascertaining the date of Monk's vision of the "age" and "beard" of Saint Patrick, we cannot fix upon her age at the time her appearance on the stage of horrors is "disclosed." Monk, it is stated, was at school when Saint Patrick was "an old woman for a nun;" but was this five or ten years ago, no reader of the "Disclosures" may say. In the meantime the "old woman" is now in her *twenty-seventh year*! [148] (italics in original)

In making the above statement, the Jesuits confirmed that in fact there was a nun in the Hotel Dieu Nunnery named Saint Patrick, who they emphatically stated was 27 years old. Mr. Smith points out that Sainte Frances Patrick told him that she was 27 years old. Mr. Smith reveals that the Jesuit book, *Awful Exposure*, was published after Sainte Frances Patrick left the nunnery and after she had revealed her age to him.

Mr. Smith concluded that the Jesuit's reference to the 27 year-old Saint Patrick who was "one of the sisterhood" was a reference to the same 27 year-old Sainte Frances Patrick he interviewed. Mr. Smith stated that Sainte Frances Patrick could not have been influenced by the Jesuit book when telling him her age, because she told him her age before she had seen or even heard of the Jesuit book. Indeed, she could not have seen or heard of it, because it was not published until after she had met and spoken with Mr. Smith. Mr. Smith's conclusion: "How striking! And what strong corroboration of the truth!"[149]

20 Masonic Secret Agent

William L. Stone was a nominal Protestant, but he was not a true believer in Jesus Christ. Indeed, he may have been a secret Catholic sympathizer. Stone was the first superintendent of public schools in New York City. In his capacity as superintendent, he was allegedly considering using bibles in the public schools. Did he confer with the pastors of the Presbyterian Church, of which he was a member? No, he did not. Did he confer with the Protestant bible societies? No, he did not do that either. He instead conferred with a representative of an organization that thinks it is dangerous for the common man to read the bible. He conferred with the Roman Catholic Archbishop of New York, John Hughes. Conferring with an enemy of the bible is no way to get bibles into schools. Stone was portraying himself as a Protestant; his conduct of conferring with the Roman Catholic archbishop allows us to see a little of his wolf's fur beneath his sheep's clothing and his affinity for the Catholic Church.

Conferring with the Catholic archbishop about bibles is really only a hint of his fidelity to Rome. There is more. Another notable fact about Stone is that he was a Freemason. He later allegedly disavowed Freemasonry, because it became politically inexpedient to be a Freemason after the infamous Captain Morgan murder. Morgan was murdered by Freemasons for revealing Masonic secrets. It seems that Stone's disavowal of Freemasonry was, like so many others, only a pretended disavowal.

Stone's opinion on the uprightness of Freemasons in their obligation to keep their oaths is still cited today in the authoritative *Mackey's Encyclopedia of Freemasonry*.[150] Would Freemasons cite Stone as an authority on Freemasonry if he had truly disavowed Freemasonry?

Stone's opinion on Masonic oaths, which is cited by *Mackey's Encyclopedia of Freemasonry*, was written by Stone after he allegedly left Freemasonry. His opinion on Masonic oaths was in the form of a letter to John Quincy Adams. That letter was originally published by Stone in his 1832 book titled: *Letters on Freemasonry and Anti-Freemasonry Addressed to the Honorable John Quincy Adams*. Stone's letter is not a condemnation of Freemasonry, but rather extols the (fictional) virtues of Freemasonry.

Stone opens that letter with the claim that "in behalf of all those virtuous and intelligent citizens with whom I have formerly associated as a Mason, utterly to disclaim any and all constructions of those obligations, at variance with the laws of God or man, or which conflict with a proper discharge of all moral, social, and religious duties of life."[151] Does that sound like a man who has truly disavowed Freemasonry? It sounds more like an advocate on behalf of Freemasonry. It is an age-old strategy to feign disavowal of membership in an organization as a way to lead the opposition to it and thereby undermine the effectiveness of that opposition. Stone as a supposed opponent of Freemasonry would be in the perfect position to limit the damage done to Freemasonry by the exposure of its secrets by Captain Morgan and the public uproar that ensued from his murder in consequence thereof. In the intelligence community this is called a "limited hangout," where certain information is acknowledged in a pretended opposition, in order to steer the opposition away from the whole truth that would damage the enterprise. Vladimir Lenin explained: "The best way to control the opposition is to lead it ourselves."

The letter written by Stone claims that the oaths of Masons do not mean what they say. One of the oaths in question, which is among the milder oaths, is the oath of the Master Mason, which Stone quotes: "Further do I promise and swear, that a Master Mason's secrets, given to me in charge as such, shall remain as secure and inviolable in my breast as in his own, when communicated to me, murder and treason excepted; and they left to my own election."[152] Stone claims that the last seven words of the oath are unfamiliar to him, and he further alleges that the oath does not allow a Mason to conceal the villainy of a fellow Mason. Stone states that "he is expressly to understand that nothing therein contained is to interfere with his political or religious principles; with his duty to God; or the laws of his country."[153] That is not true, and Stone knew it when he wrote it. In fact, the whole point of the oath is to keep the villainy of fellow Masons secret. Why else would there be mention of the specific crimes of murder and treason in the oath if it were not to cover for the villainy of fellow Freemasons? The *Handbook of Masonry* states flat out that a Mason must even commit perjury if necessary to conceal the crimes of a fellow Mason.[154] The blood oaths of fidelity to the secrets of Masonry were seen in operation by the obstruction of justice by Freemasons during the investigation into the Morgan murder. Stone, by his dissimulation, has impeached his credibility and revealed himself as a deceiving apologist for the Freemasons, while pretending to oppose them.

One might ask what is wrong with being a Freemason? Isn't Freemasonry just a fraternal organization? Freemasonry is a heathen religion. There is not only a link between Islam and Catholicism, but there is also a clear link between Islam and Freemasonry, and a link between Catholicism and Freemasonry. Indeed, the Vatican has a pattern of using Protestant Masons as its undercover agents. Freemason Billy Graham is probably the most famous example of that phenomenon. Graham's covert activities on behalf of the Vatican are detailed in this author's book, *The Anti-Gospel*.

James D. Shaw was the first to authoritatively expose Billy Graham's Masonic membership. Shaw was a former Freemason. He attained the rank of a 33rd Degree Freemason, Knight Commander of the Court of Honor, Past Worshipful Master, Blue Lodge, and Past Master of all Scottish Rite Bodies. Shaw was saved by the grace of God, left Freemasonry, and wrote a book titled *The Deadly Deception*. Shaw revealed that Billy Graham personally attended Shaw's ceremony of induction as a 33rd degree Mason. Only fellow 33rd degree Masons are allowed to attend such ceremonies.

Albert Pike, the theological pontiff of Freemasonry, stated that the root of Freemasonry is that the god of Freemasonry is Lucifer.[155] Martin L. Wagner conducted an objective and thorough study of Freemasonry and wrote a book about his findings titled *Freemasonry: An Interpretation*. Wagner's authoritative study of Freemasonry concludes that Freemasonry is not simply a fraternal organization, it is in fact a religion. What kind of religion is Masonry? Wagner interviewed many former Masons who quit Masonry because they discovered that the Masonic religion was antithetical to Christianity. "Its aim and tendency is to undermine their faith in the Lord Jesus Christ as their personal Saviour; that it alienates their affections and support from the church, and destroys their faith in the Bible as the word of God."[156]

The god of Freemasonry is the Great Architect of the Universe. In order to keep up the charade that the Masonic Great Architect of the Universe is the God of the bible, Freemasons conceal from the public the name of their god. Freemasons call their Great Architect of the Universe by the name *Jabulun*[157] (a/k/a *Jah-Bul-On*[158] or *Jah-Bel-On*[159]). That name is a cryptographic word that is based upon the abbreviated names for Jehovah (*Jah*), Baal (*Bel* or *Bul*), and Osiris (*On*).[160] The Freemasons blasphemously identify Jehovah, who is the God of the bible, as the Hebrew sun god.[161] The Freemasons join that name to Baal, who was the Assyrian sun god, to whom the Jews sacrificed their children. *See* Jeremiah 32:26-36. The sixteenth century demonologist John Weir identified Baal as a devil.[162] Osiris was the Egyptian sun god. There cannot be a joining of God with Baal, Osiris, or any other heathen god. "What concord hath Christ with Belial?" 2 Corinthians 6:15. The Prophet Elijah stated "if the Lord be God, follow him: but if Baal, then follow him." 1 Kings 18:21. There is only one God and salvation is solely by the grace of God through faith in Jesus Christ. "Neither is there salvation in any other: for there is none other name under heaven given among men, whereby we must be saved" Acts 4:12.

The cryptic title for the god of the Masons acts as a glyph to conceal the true god of Freemasonry, who is Lucifer. The Supreme Theological Pontiff of Freemasonry, Albert Pike, said that "[t]he doctrine of Satanism is heresy; and the true and pure philosophic religion is the belief in Lucifer, the equal of Adonay; but Lucifer, God of Light and God of Good, is struggling for humanity against Adonay, the God of Darkness and Evil."[163] The doctrines of Freemasonry are influenced to a great extent by Roman Catholic doctrine and history. In 1754 the first 25 degrees of the Scottish Rite of Freemasonry were written by the Jesuits in the College of Jesuits of Clermont in Paris, for the purpose of restoring to power the Jesuit controlled House of Stuart to the throne of England.[164] There are a series of degrees in the Masonic York Rite hierarchy known as the Order of Knights Templar. The Knights Templar was an organization founded in 1118 A.D. The Templars received papal sanction as a Catholic order (the Order of the Poor Knights of Christ) in 1128 and are recognized as the first Roman Catholic crusaders. The Templars were known as the "Militia of Christ." As explained by Nesta Webster, Freemasonry is an amalgam of the theology and secret practices of the Roman Catholic Templars and Cabalistic Jews.[165] Freemasonry is a phallic religion, like Islam and Catholicism. For more information on Freemasonry read this author's book, *Bloody Zion*.

Was William L. Stone's tour of the Montreal nunnery and pretended refutation of Maria Monk a fulfilment of his masonic blood oath of deception? The initiation into the Royal Arch (7th degree of the York Rite and 13th degree of the Scottish Rite) requires the initiate to drink wine from the top half of a human skull and take a blood oath not to reveal any of the secrets of Masonry and to lie and do anything else necessary to assist a fellow Mason in extricating himself from the consequences of committing any crime, including murder and treason. The *Handbook of Masonry* states that a Mason "must conceal all the crimes of your brother Masons ... and should you be summoned as a witness against a brother Mason be always sure to shield him ... It may be perjury to do this, it is true, but you're keeping your obligations."[166] According to the Roman Catholic publication Sodalitium, in 1961, Pope John XXIII reinstated the Knights of Malta and rescinded the prohibition of Roman Catholics holding membership in Freemasonry.[167]

While Pope John XXIII's edict was the first public permission given for Roman Catholics to become Freemasons, there were many Freemasons within the Catholic hierarchy for hundreds years prior to that, during which time there had been secret intercourse and cooperation. One notable Catholic Freemason was Pope John XXIII himself. French Freemason, Baron Yves Marsaudon, revealed that Roncalli (later elected Pope John XXIII) became a 33rd degree Freemason while a papal nuncio to France, between 1944 and 1953. During that time, Catholics were supposed to be prohibited from membership in Freemasonry. Baron Marsaudon was appointed by Pope John XXIII as head of the French branch of the Knights of Malta.[168] The fact that Pope John XXIII was a Freemason was confirmed by the Grand Master of the Grand Orient of Italy, who said in an interview for *30 Days* magazine: "As for that, it seems that John XXIII was initiated (into a Masonic lodge) in Paris and participated in the work of the Istanbul workshops."[169] (parenthetical in original)

Former Jesuit priest Alberto Rivera testified to the cooperation between the Jesuits and Freemasons. In one instance, Rivera was invited by high ranking Jesuit officials to a secret black Mass in Spain. At the event, River kneeled in obeisance to kiss a Jesuit official's ring.[170] The ring he kissed bore a Masonic symbol, indicating that the Jesuit official was a Freemason.

Could Stone have been a Freemason on a secret assignment in service of Rome when he was given the tour of the Montreal nunnery? It is notable that Stone was one of very few persons who was ever allowed by the Catholic bishop inside the cloistered area of the nunnery to be given permission by the Catholic bishop to publish what he saw. That fact alone makes the whole affair suspicious. The Bishop refused all requests by Maria Monk to be allowed to bring in objective observers. Why was not Maria Monk, along with people of her choosing, allowed to tour the nunnery and document the event, as she requested? The answer is obvious. The whole point of Stone's tour was not to reveal but to conceal. As much as the Catholic authorities tried to rearrange the nunnery with new construction, they could not rebuild the building. They could not allow Monk to guide people to secret passages and to areas of the nunnery that only one who resided there would know about. Her knowledge of the building could have exposed the new construction.

After Stone's Article refuting Maria Monk appeared, a Protestant organization published a booklet, titled: *Evidence Demonstrating the Falsehoods of William L. Stone Concerning the Hotel Dieu Nunnery of Montreal*. That booklet reveals that while Stone publically maintained that his article was an accurate representation of what he saw at the nunnery, he had privately confessed that his article was a deception.[171]

Stone's mission to Montreal from the beginning was designed to refute the charges of Maria Monk. When Maria Monk first went public with her story, Stone's newspaper, the *New York Commercial Advertiser*, initially published articles in support of Maria Monk. However, because of pressure from some subscribers in Canada who cancelled subscriptions, and fearing the lost income from further cancellations, Stone's newspaper did an about face and changed its stance regarding Maria Monk. Stone's newspaper went from supporting Monk to suddenly calling her book "a humbug."[172] Stone came to understand clearly that his Canadian subscribers were under the influence of the Catholic prelates, most of whom would cancel their subscriptions if ordered by them to do so. Stone's mission to tour the Hotel Dieu Nunnery in Montreal was for the purpose of placating the Catholic prelates and preventing his Catholic Canadian subscribers from cancelling their subscriptions.[173]

21 A U.S. Senator Defends Maria Monk

Maria Monk gave specific names of nuns and priests and alleged they committed murder, torture, and rape in a nunnery under the auspices of the Roman Catholic Church. One would think that if her claims were false, that the nuns, priests and the Roman Church would bring a libel action in court against her and her publisher. In fact, she challenged the Catholic Church to do just that. Yet the Catholic Church and its nuns and priests did not dare bring a suit in court against Maria Monk or her publisher. That is because the truth is a complete defense in a libel case. Furthermore, there is something called "discovery" in civil litigation that would allow the opposing party to demand witnesses be subpoenaed and questioned under oath in depositions, as well as at the actual trial. The trial testimony and depositions would be stenographically recorded and made public. A deposition is no simple affidavit. During a deposition a witness is questioned in detail by the attorneys for both parties. The Catholic Church simply could not allow that to happen. The Catholic Church, however, to this day is desperate to conceal Maria Monk's revelations. So desperate is the Roman Catholic hierarchy to keep a lid on her revelations that they have gone on record to claim that Maria Monk never existed. Indeed, U.S. Senator Thomas E. Watson reveals that on or before 1923 "a Romanist and Jesuit— one M. J. Walsh, of Augusta, Georgia— roundly asserted in a recent issue of The Sunday Visitor, a leading Catholic paper, that 'There never was a Maria Monk case!'"[174]

Here we have the largest Catholic periodical in the country, *The Sunday Visitor*, allege that Maria Monk never existed. However, over the years, the Roman Catholic hierarchy has admitted her existence. In fact, Maria Monk's existence is a prerequisite to the Catholic assassination of her character. How can the Catholic Church portray her as both non-existent and a liar at the same time? It is impossible.

Indeed, the Jesuits have implicitly acknowledged Maria Monk's existence by putting up a woman, who alleged that she was Maria Monk's daughter, to write a libelous book about Maria Monk. It is not clear whether the author was actually Maria Monk's daughter; what is clear from reading the book, is that the author was an ardent Roman Catholic who was completely under the beguiling superstitious influence of the Roman Catholic Church. U.S. Senator Thomas E. Watson had this to say about the book written by Maria Monk's alleged daughter.

> Too astute and too cowardly to prosecute the Harper Brothers [publishers of Maria Monk's book, Awful Disclosures] and Maria Monk, the priests took up the

weapons of Jesuitism.

A bulky book called "Maria Monk's Daughter," was published in New York by the U. S. Publishing Co.— whatever that concern may have been. It was probably a nice, patriotic name to cover a Roman Catholic publisher. In this volume, a "Mrs. L. St. John Eckel," strives to show up her own mother, as an imposter and a bawd!

The loyal Daughter says in her story that she wrote her book at the command of a priest. This admission, of course, puts the royal o. k. on the work.

The Eckel woman asserts that Maria Monk was Mrs. St. John, and says of her. "She was my mother, and I hated her."

The narrative of Mrs. Eckel is so confused, and so very much in contrast to the simple clearness of Maria Monk's, that it is difficult to follow and untangle her statements. ...

There are many omissions in the "Maria Monk's Daughter" which cannot be explained. It is not stated when, where and of what parentage, "mother" was born; it is not stated when, where, and under what circumstances, "mother" was married to St. John; it is not stated when, where, and how "mother" misbehaved herself; it is not stated when, by whom, and what evidence, "mother" was sentenced to Blackwell's Island. It is not stated that the "Daughter" was present when "mother" was tried, nor that the Daughter ever visited the imprisoned mother; nor that the Daughter knew when her mother died, how she died, and where she was buried.

It is not stated where, when, and in what circumstances "father" died, although the Daughter was ravenously fond of "father." It is not stated who were the neighbors and the barkeepers who knew of "mother's" dissolute habits.

Great pains are taken to embellish Daughter's book with a picture of her own lovable self, and of several hard-faced, nutcracker aunts of hers; but no picture of father or mother is presented. In fact, there is the strangest avoidance of names, dates, and corroborating incidents, the very things so necessary to be a book of this character.

The mother's narrative was published in 1836; the Daughter's attack, in 1874: the prudent priests and the dutiful Daughter patiently waited 38 years before assailing the dead.

A good many witnesses can die, disappear, or be silenced in 38 years. Against the dead woman were the organizations of the most powerful and criminal church that ever cursed the world: in favor of the dead, there was nothing, save the intrinsic evidences of truth borne in her plain, connected, circumstantial narrative, supplemented by the affidavits of a few persons who knew Maria Monk, but who could not possibly know what had been done to her in the Nunnery. ...

As I have indicated, there is not a single shred of evidence produced in this vile book to support its statements. No letter of corroboration, no affidavit, no document, no transcript from any record.

It will occur to every intelligent reader that the very first requisites to such a work as that of "Maria Monk's Daughter" would have been a transcript of the court sentence which condemned Maria Monk to Blackwell's Island, and a transcript from the books kept there, to show what became of her. No such documentary evidence has yet been forthcoming. Nor has anyone ever produced an affidavit, from neighbor, bar-keeper, brothel-keeper, or others, to substantiate the charge that Maria Monk was a drunkard and a prostitute.

It must be clear to you that the Harper Brothers did not assume the risks and responsibilities of such a book as the "Awful Disclosures" without having made careful inquiries into her antecedents. If the book had been a tissue of falsehoods, the Harper Brothers could have been ruined by libel suits and prosecutions.

It must be equally clear to you that if Maria Monk afterwards became a drunkard and a prostitute, her persecutors would have gathered up affidavits by the dozen, and published them at that time.[175]

When the world's most powerful religious and political institution makes a special project of ruining a person, can there be any doubt that they could do just that and even drive that person mad? Senator Watson points out that "they hounded her, with the cowardice and savagery of wolves; they slandered her and isolated her; they terrorized the poor creature so ruthlessly and persistently."[176]

The manifold way in which the Jesuits carried out their destruction of Maria Monk's character caused them to make mistakes in their tapestry of dissemblance. For example, the false affidavit of one Mrs. Tarbert claimed that Maria Monk was working as a prostitute in a Montreal brothel in the summer of 1835. Tarbert's affidavit contradicts the false affidavit of Maria Monk's mother, who claimed that Maria Monk, during that period, had traveled from New York to Montreal to see her with her five week old child, accompanied by a Mr. Hoyte. Senator Watson explains:

> Mrs. Monk is flatly contradicted by Mrs. Tarbert, for if Maria was the inmate of a

brothel in Montreal, the Summer of 1835, her mother could not have truthfully sworn that she came from New York, with Hoyte, the same Summer![177]

There can be no confusion in dates. There is internal verification of the dates of the two affidavits that locks in the contradiction; that is the age of Maria Monk's baby. Senator Watson explains:

> There is one fact which proves that Mrs. Tarbert meant the Spring and Summer of 1835: it is the age of the baby!
>
> Old Mrs. Monk swears that "in August, 1835," the child of Maria was five weeks old; and Mrs. Tarbert swears that she knew Maria was with child in the Spring and Summer. Then, necessarily, it was the Spring and Summer of 1835.
>
> But what was Maria doing in a brothel when so near confinement? and how did she go from Montreal to New York, strike up with Hoyte, and reappear at Montreal with a five-weeks baby in August?[178]

Maria Monk's revelations created a sensation. Many wanted to get to the bottom of the matter and determine the truth. A group of Protestants published a challenge to the Catholic hierarchy to set up an assembly to impartially examine the evidence. Senator Watson describes the challenge.

The Protestant Vindicator of New York, took up the cause of the persecuted woman, and published a challenge to the very priests whose names had been mentioned by Maria Monk. That dare to the Romanists appeared on April 6, 1836.

It was addressed to the Roman Prelate and Priests of Montreal — Messrs. Conroy, Quarter and Schneller, of New York — Messrs. Fenwick and Byrne, of Boston — Mr. Hughes, of Philadelphia—the Arch-Prelate of Baltimore, and his subordinate priests, and also to Bishop England, of Charleston, South Carolina.

The terms of the challenge were :

"To meet an investigation of the truth of Maria Monk's 'Awful Disclosures,' before an impartial assembly, over which shall preside seven gentlemen; three to be selected by the Roman priests, three by the executive committee of the New York Protestant Association, and the seventh as chairman to be chosen by the six.

"An eligible place in New York shall be appointed and the regulations for the decorum and order of the meetings with all the other arrangements, shall be made by the above gentlemen.

"All communications upon this subject

from any of the Roman priests or nuns, either individually, or as delegates for their superiors, addressed to the Corresponding Secretary of the New York Protestant Association, No. 142 Nassau Street. New York, will be promptly answered."

This challenge was published for several weeks, and nobody ventured to accept it. Afraid of a show-down, afraid to meet the woman they had so foully wronged, the Romanists slunk back in guilty silence, preferring to trust to their favorite weapons, slanders, abuse, falsehoods, denials, and defamation of character.[179]

Nothing was ever heard from the accused Roman Catholic priests and nuns in response to the quite reasonable challenge. It is truly strange that any person or organization accused of such abominable crimes as alleged by Maria Monk would pass up an opportunity to prove the falsity of the claims; particularly, when the very organization had so vehemently denied the truth of the allegations. The resolute refusal of the Catholic hierarchy to take advantage of such an opportunity strongly suggests that the allegations are true and their refusal to seek redress is out of fear that any objective review of the facts would prove the allegations to be true. The *Protestant Vindicator* responded in an editorial to the refusal of the Catholic Church to avail itself of an opportunity to refute though evidence the allegations of Maria Monk.

THE CHALLENGE. — We have been waiting with no small degree of impatience to hear from some of the Roman priests. But neither they, nor their sisters, the nuns, nor one of their nephews or nieces, have yet ventured to come out. Our longings meet only with disappointment. Did ever any person hear of similar conduct on the part of men accused of the highest crimes, in their deepest dye? Here is a number of Roman priests, as actors, or accessories, openly denounced before the world as guilty of the most outrageous sins against the sixth and seventh commandments. They are charged before the world with adultery, fornication, and murder! The allegations are distinctly made, the place is mentioned, the parties are named, and the time is designated; for it is lasting as the annual revolutions of the seasons. And what is most extraordinary — the highest official authorities in Canada know that all these statements are true, and they sanction and connive at the iniquity! The priests and nuns have been offered, for several months past, the most easy and certain mode to disprove the felonies imputed to them, and they are still as the dungeons of the inquisition, silent as the death-like quietude of the Convent cell; and as retired as if they were in the subterraneous passages between the Nunnery and Lartique's habitation. Now, we contend, that scarcely a similar instance of disregard for the opinions of mankind, can be found since the Reformation, at least, in a Protestant country. Whatever disregard for the judgment of others the Romish priests may have felt, where the inquisition was at their command, and the civil power was their Jackal and their Hyena, they have been obliged to pay some little regard to the opinion of Protestants, and to the dread of exposure. We therefore repeat the solemn indubitable truth — that the facts which are stated by Maria Monk, respecting the Hotel Dieu Nunnery at Montreal, are true as the existence of the priests and nuns — that the character, principles, and practices of the Jesuits and nuns in Canada are most accurately delineated — that popish priests, and sisters of charity in the United States, are their faithful and exact counterparts — that many female schools in the United States, kept by the papist teachers, are nothing more than places of decoy through which young women, at the most delicate age, are ensnared into the power of the Roman priests — that the toleration of the monastic system in the United States and Britain, the only two countries in the world in which that unnatural abomination is now extending its withering influence, is high treason against God and mankind. If American citizens and British Christians, after the appalling developments which have been made, permit the continuance of that prodigious wickedness which is inseparable from Nunneries and the celibacy of popish priests, they will ere long experience that divine castigation which is justly due to transgressors who wilfully trample upon all the appointments of God, and who subvert the foundation of national concord and extinguish the comforts of domestic society. Listen to the challenge again! All the papers with which the Protestant Vindicator exchanges are requested to give the challenge one, or more than one, insertion.[180]

22   The Torture Room

Below is an excerpt from the 1858 book written by Sarah J. Richardson, *Life in the Grey Nunnery at Montreal*. Like Maria Monk, she was one of the few nuns to successfully escape from a cloistered nunnery and live to tell about it. The shocking revelations in the book are supported by six affidavits appended to the book attesting to the veracity and honesty of Sarah J. Richardson. Indeed, Sarah Richardson, herself, appended an affidavit to the book swearing under oath to its truth. She stated in pertinent part: "I, Sarah J. Richardson ... do solemnly swear, declare and say, that the foregoing pages contain a true and faithful history of my life before my marriage to the said Frederick S. Richardson, and that every statement made herein by me is true."[181]

The veracity of Sarah Richardson is significantly enhanced by the fact that she resisted every effort to convince her to publish her account of her life in the Grey

Nunnery. She was afraid of certain death that would be orchestrated by the Romish priests. She stated: "For my life I would not do it. Not because I do not wish the world to know it, for I would gladly proclaim it wherever a Romanist is known, but it would be impossible for me to escape their hands should I make myself so public. They would most assuredly take my life."[182] Once she was married, however, she felt protected by her husband and therefore felt free to publicly reveal in a book the horrors of the Grey Nunnery.

In addition to all of the other abuse that Sarah endured at the nunnery, she was one day sent to a torture room that was concealed in the bowels of the nunnery. Sarah made a trifling mistake for which she was to be punished. The pertinent part of her punishment required her to spend three days in a torture room. Until she was escorted to the torture room, she did not know that the room even existed at the nunnery. Sarah stated that the entrance to the torture room was so well hidden in the cellar of the nunnery that one could spend a lifetime in the nunnery and not know of its existence. Below is a narrative from chapter 17 of her book that recounts what Sarah saw in the torture room:

> I remember hearing a gentleman at the depot remark that the very enormity of the crimes committed by the Romanists, is their best protection. "For," said he, "some of their practices are so shockingly infamous they may not even be alluded to in the presence of the refined and the virtuous. And if the story of their guilt were told, who would believe the tale? Far easier

would it be to call the whole a slanderous fabrication, than to believe that man can be so vile." This consideration led me to doubt the propriety of attempting a description of what I saw in that room. But I have engaged to give a faithful narrative of what transpired in the nunnery; and shall I leave out a part because it is so strange and monstrous, that people will not believe it? No. I will tell, without the least exaggeration what I saw, heard, and experienced. People may not credit the story now, but a day will surely come when they will know that I speak the truth.

As I entered the room I was exceedingly shocked at the horrid spectacle that met my eye. I knew that fearful scenes were enacted in the subterranean cells, but I never imagined anything half so terrible as this. In various parts of the room I saw machines, and instruments of torture, and on some of them persons were confined who seemed to be suffering the most excruciating agony. I paused, utterly overcome with terror, and for a moment imagined that I was a witness to the torments, which, the priests say, are endured by the lost, in the world of woe. Was I to undergo such tortures, and which of those infernal engines would be applied to me? I was not long in doubt. The priest took hold of me and put me into a machine that held me fast, while my feet rested on a piece of iron which was gradually heated until both feet were blistered. I think I must have been there fifteen minutes, but perhaps the time seemed longer than it was. He then took me out, put some ointment on my feet and left me.

I was now at liberty to examine more minutely the strange objects around me. There were some persons in the place whose punishment, like my own, was light compared with others. But near me lay one old lady extended on a rack. Her joints were all dislocated, and she was emaciated to the last degree. I do not suppose I can describe this rack, for I never saw anything like it. It looked like a gridiron but was long enough for the tallest man to lie upon. There were large rollers at each end, to which belts were attached, with a large lever to drive them back and forth. Upon this rack the poor woman was fastened in such a way, that when the levers were turned and the rollers made to revolve, every bone in her body was displaced. Then the violent strain would be relaxed, a little, and she was so very poor, her skin would sink into the joints and remain there till it mortified and corrupted.

It was enough to melt the hardest heart to witness her agony; but she bore it with a degree of fortitude and patience, I could not have supposed possible, had I not been compelled to behold it. When I entered the room she looked up and said, "Have you come to release me, or only to suffer with me?" I did not dare to reply, for the priest was there, but when he left us she exclaimed, "My child, let nothing induce you to believe this cursed religion. It will be the death of you, and that death, will be the death of a dog." I suppose she meant that they would kill me as they would a dog. She then asked, "Who put you here?" "My Father," said I. "He must have been a brute," said she, "or he never could have done it." At one time I happened to mention the name of God, when she fiercely exclaimed with gestures of contempt, "A God! You believe there is one, do you? Don't you suffer yourself to believe any such thing. Think you that a wise, merciful, and all powerful being would allow such a hell as this to exist? Would he suffer me to be torn from friends and home, from my poor children and all that my soul holds dear, to be confined in this den of iniquity, and tortured to death in this cruel manner? No, O, no. He would at once destroy these monsters in human form; he would not suffer them, for one moment, to breathe the pure air of heaven."

At another time she exclaimed, "O, my children! my poor motherless children! What will become of them? God of mercy, protect my children!" Thus, at one moment, she would say there was no God, and the next, pray to him for help. This did not surprise me, for she was in such intolerable misery she did not realize what she did say. Every few hours the priest came in, and gave the rollers a turn, when her joints would crack and--but I cannot describe it. The sight made me sick and faint at the time, as the recollection of it, does now. It seemed as though that man must have had a heart of adamant, or he could not have done it. She would shriek, and groan, and weep, but it did not affect him in the least. He was as calm, and deliberate as though he had a block of wood in his hands, instead of a human being. When I saw him coming, I once shook my head at her, to have her stop speaking; but when he was gone, she said, "Don't shake your head at me; I do not fear him. He can but kill me, and the quicker he does it the better. I would be glad if he would put an end to my misery at once, but that would be too merciful. He is determined to kill me by inches, and it makes no difference what I say to him."

She had no food, or drink, during the three days I was there, and the priest never spoke to her. He brought me my bread and water regularly, and I would gladly have given it to that poor woman if she would have taken it. But she would not accept the offer. It would only prolong her sufferings, and she wished to die. I do not suppose she could have lived, had she been taken out when I first saw her.

In another part of the room, a monk was under punishment. He was standing in some kind of a machine, with heavy weights attached to his feet, and a belt passed across his breast under his arms. He appeared to be in great distress, and no refreshment was furnished him while I was there.

On one side of the room, I observed a closet with a "slide door," as the nuns called them. There were several doors of this description in the building, so constructed as to slide back into the ceiling out of sight. Through this opening I could see an image resembling a monk; and whenever any one was put in there, they would shriek, and groan, and beg to be taken out, but I could not ascertain the cause of their suffering.

One day a nun was brought in to be punished. The priest led her up to the side of the room, and bade her put her fingers into some holes in the wall just large enough to admit them. She obeyed but immediately drew them back with a loud shriek. I looked to see what was the matter with her, and lo! every nail was torn from her fingers, which were bleeding profusely.

How it was done, I do not know. Certainly, there was no visible cause for such a surprising effect. In all probability the fingers came in contact with the spring of some machine on the other side, or within the wall to which some sharp instrument was attached. I would give much to know just how it was constructed, and what the girl had done to subject herself to such a terrible and unheard-of punishment. But this, like many other things in that establishment, was wrapped in impenetrable mystery. God only knows when the veil will be removed, or whether it ever will be until the day when all secret things will be brought to light.[183]

23 The Abuse of Nuns Continues

Maria Monk was not an isolated historical anomaly; the sexual abuse of nuns by priests has spanned the centuries. Peter de Rosa in his book, *Vicars of Christ*, concluded that "[a] large part of the history of celibacy is the story of the degradation of women and – an invariable consequence – frequent abortions and infanticide. In the ninth century, many monasteries were the haunts of homosexuals; many convents were brothels in which babies were killed and buried. ... Promiscuity was rife in monasteries and convents. The great Ivo of Chartres (1040-1115) tells of whole convents with inmates who were nuns only in name. They had often been abandoned by their families and were really prostitutes."[184]

'Sister Jesme,' in her 2009 book, *The Autobiography of a Nun*, not only reveals fornication between priests and nuns, but also predatory lesbianism within the walls of Catholic convents.[185]

Former Catholic priest Shibu Kalamparambil, in

his 2010 memoir *Oru Vaidikante Hrudayamitha (The Heart of a Priest)*, states:

> The convents and nunneries are being converted into brothels. The priests have sex with the nuns at night in these convents. Because of these acts, the chastity of the priests and nuns has come under suspicion. Their love for God has shrunk...some of the clergy protect their chastity by watching pornography and reading pornographic material. They lose themselves in this habit. These books and DVDs are kept in secret places and can't be found easily.[186]

Sister Mary Chandy corroborates the statements of the former priest. Sister Chandy fled a Catholic convent in India after 40 years as a nun. In 2012, Sister Mary Chandy stated in an interview that "most often, priests and nuns fail to keep their vows of chastity ... Those who refuse to succumb are viciously targeted."[187] Sister Chandy explained the sexual exploitation:

> It was the life there, which was more inclined towards lust than the spirituality, which made her leave the convents forever, she writes. Those nuns who did not submit to the lustful moves of the priests were often targeted and their life was made a hell, says the former nun. In one chapter she even narrates how a priest tried to rape her and she escaped the attempt by hitting him with a stool. But there again she was

branded a misfit for serving the church and the convent, she says.[188]

Sister Chandy wrote a book in 2012 titled: *Nanma Niranjavale Swasthi (Peace to the One filled with Grace)*. In the book, Sister Chandy revealed that "abortions are commonplace in convents."[189] Sister Chandy further tells how she witnessed an attempt by a priest and nun to kill a newborn baby. Sister Chandy was able to intervene and save the child, which she subsequently delivered to an orphanage.[190] Sister Chandy explained the harrowing experience:

> The cry of a baby came from the bathroom of one of the inner rooms along with the sobs of a woman. We used our might to force open the bathroom door and what we saw would break anyone's heart. A nun who had given birth to a child was pushing the head of the baby into the closet [i.e., toilet]. The bathroom was filled with blood. The legs of the child, which were sticking out of the closet, were kicking for life. ... After I broke open the door with the help of another nun, I grabbed the child and held it to my chest. I thought I was doing the right thing but the sisters turned against me. I want to know why. In a previous incident, when I hit a priest on his head with a stool when he tried to grab me, the nuns sympathized with the priest. From then on, I was watched carefully.[191]

The superstitions of the monastic life had so seared

the consciences of the nuns and priests that they viewed Sister Chandy's noble act of saving the baby from being murdered and her successful effort in fending off the attempts of a priest to rape her as misbehavior within the convent.

As they did with Maria Monk, the Roman Catholic Church denied that Sister Chandy was ever a nun. The Catholic authorities claim that Sister Chandy was only a kitchen maid in the convent.

The odd thing is that the Catholic Church has reportedly mobilized a fact-finding team to investigate the allegations made by Sister Chandy. "The team had been to several spots mentioned in the book and otherwise, to collect evidence. The church is planning to come out with the facts soon, it is learned."[192] Why would the Catholic Church send out a fact-finding team, if Sister Chandy was never a nun and was only a kitchen maid? If they are certain that she is a fraud who is only portraying herself as a nun, why investigate the specific facts? It makes no sense, unless the fact-finding team is actually a cover-up team mobilized to conduct damage control. That seems to be the case; in over two years since the alleged fact-finding mission was instituted, the promised report has never materialized.

Chandy has stated that her ghost writer, Jose Pazhookkaran, demanded money from her when the book became a success, but that she refused his demands. When Sister Chandy refused his demand, the ghost writer came forward to parrot the allegations of the Catholic Church. Jose Pazhookkaran alleged that "after the book was released, I got numerous telephone calls stating that she was never a nun, but a helper in the kitchen of a convent."[193] Pazhookkaran stated that he was shocked and investigated the allegations "and found out that she was telling wrong things."[194]

Suspiciously, Pazhookkaran never explained what those "wrong things" were. He gave no details as to what he found during his alleged investigation. Pazhookkaran contacted the publisher to withdraw the book. However, the publisher was unconvinced by Pazhookkaran's allegations. The publisher had a significant interest in heeding Pazshookkaran's demand, since the publisher would be now be exposed to a libel judgment on behalf of the Roman Catholic Church, if Pazhookkaran's claims were true. The fact that the publisher refused to withdraw the book, speaks loudly to the baselessness of his claims. If the claims by Pazhookkaran had any merit, the publisher would have certainly withdrawn the book.

The basis of Pazhookkaran's claim was the same as the basis for the Roman Catholic claim: that Chandy was not a nun, but rather a kitchen maid at the convent. If that was the case, the proof is entirely within the hands of the Roman Catholic Church. If Chandy was a kitchen maid, that means that she was a hired worker, who was paid wages. That in turn means that there would be records of the wages paid to her for her services. All the Catholic Church needs to do is produce those records and that would prove their case and destroy the credibility of Sister Chandy. It has now been over two years since her book was published in 2012, and no records have been produced. Indeed, it is fair to say that no records will ever be produced, because if such records existed, they would certainly have been made public. Such proof would almost certainly be shared with Pazhookkaran, if the Catholic Church had it to share. Not a peep has been heard from either the Catholic Church or Pazhookkaran regarding employment records or any other proof that she was a kitchen maid as they claim.

Indeed, the absence of an entry in a record of regularly conducted business activity, is admissible evidence in most courts to prove that the activity did not take place.[195] The absence of any employment records for Sister Chandy as a kitchen maid is evidence that she was not a kitchen maid, as claimed by the Catholic Church and Pazhookkaran. The contrary inference is that she was in fact a nun, just as she claimed.

The reason the rampant infanticide is little known outside the confines of convents is explained by a child advocacy group, Child Abuse Recovery: "There was assurance from the Vatican that anyone tarnishing the Roman Catholic Church by reporting such crimes would be excommunicated and thus live in eternal Hell."[196] Occasionally, such events do leak out.

One rare case of a public revelation of infanticide took place in the 1977 case of Sister Maureen Murphy. She killed her newborn child shortly after giving birth in the Our Lady of Lourdes Convent in Brighton, New York, by stuffing clothing down his throat causing asphyxiation. The homicide came to light because Sister Maureen Murphy was found bleeding in her room by other nuns and was rushed to the hospital. The doctors determined at the hospital that the bleeding nun had just given birth to a child. Once it became known to the outside world that the nun had given birth, the nuns who accompanied her to the hospital had little choice but to return to the convent to look for the child. The dead baby boy was found by the nuns hidden in a wastebasket behind a bookcase in her room. Sister Maureen Murphy refused to disclose the name of the father of her baby. The facts were that she had resided in the convent for the entirety of the previous 19 years, and during that time the only males allowed inside the convent were Catholic priests.[197]

Sister Maureen Murphy waived her right to a jury trial and agreed to be tried before a judge, in what is known as a bench trial. Sister Maureen Murphy was found not-guilty of first degree manslaughter after a 10 day bench trial. Judge Hyman T. Maas rendered his verdict without any explanation and immediately walked off the bench.[198] It is unusual for a judge to render a verdict in a bench trial in a murder case without explaining his reasoning. It was especially unusual in a case where the circumstantial evidence was clear that the defendant killed the child. The defense was based upon two inconsistent (and easily disproved) arguments: 1) the baby was already dead upon being born, or 2) if the baby was alive, the nun was so distraught that she could not form the intent to kill the child. If the child was already dead upon birth, why would the nun bother stuffing clothing down his throat? If the nun did not have the capacity to kill the child, why would she take the extra step of hiding the dead child after killing him?

Anyone would expect those questions to be answered by a judge who had just rendered a not-guilty verdict. In fact, the judge had previously stated that he would consider lesser charges of second degree manslaughter and negligent homicide. Instead, the judge simply rendered his verdict and walked off the bench. It is truly strange for the judge to immediately exit the bench and leave the courtroom after rendering a verdict without explanation in a first degree manslaughter case, particularly when the defendant was faced with two lesser charges as possible verdicts.

Why would Judge Maas not explain the legal and factual basis for his verdict? The logical inference is that perhaps Judge Maas did not have a good legal or factual basis for his verdict. The June 14, 1972, Catholic Courier Journal, a newspaper of the Catholic Diocese of Rochester, New York, may offer some explanation for the strange behavior by the judge. The Catholic publication carried a half-page advertisement on behalf of Judge Hyman T. Maas.[199] The campaign advertisement carried a photograph of Judge Maas with the caption "Keep Judge Hy Maas County Circuit Judge."[200] It instructed the readers to: "Vote for Judge Hyman T. Maas in the Republican Primary, June 20, 1972, Pull Lever 6B."[201]

One may argue that the advertisement only evidences an effort by Judge Maas to get votes. That advertisement, however, is not a simple advertisement of a plumber in a church flyer; it is a campaign advertisement for a judge in a diocesan-wide newspaper. That advertisement shows that Judge Maas saw the advantage of currying favor with the Roman Catholic diocese and taking advantage of the large block of Catholic voters under its control.

The advertisement is evidence of the influence of the Catholic Church over Judge Maas. One may ask: what influence? The Roman Catholic Church is as much a political organization as it is a religious institution. It is an authoritarian organization, with a strict hierarchy. That advertisement would never have appeared in the diocesan newspaper without approval from the office of the Bishop of Rochester, who at the time was Joseph L. Hogan. The bishop's office would not have given its approval for the advertisement without being convinced of Hyman Maas' fidelity to the Catholic Church. The advertisement is evidence that the Catholic hierarchy was assured of Judge Maas' loyalty.

Other than the nun herself, the only other entity who would benefit directly from a not-guilty verdict was the Roman Catholic Church. A guilty verdict would have been sensational news and raised questions on just how widespread was the practice of infanticide in Catholic convents. It was a topic that the Catholic Church could not allow to be broached. The not-guilty verdict was anti-climactic and ended the public curiosity over the issue of infanticide in Catholic convents.

There is no direct evidence that the not-guilty verdict was based on anything other than the evidence in the case. However, since Judge Maas did not explain his verdict, and indeed seemed to go out of his way not to give his reasoning, it is logical to consider the possibility that Judge Maas based his decision on something other than the facts and the law in the case. Whatever was the reason for Judge Maas' decision, his strange conduct in walking off the bench without explaining his verdict causes one to reflect on the statement made by the Archbishop of New York on or about 1855 to Clarence, the attorney arguing for the release of two recaptured nuns. The Archbishop stated that "he held in his grasp the fortunes of those who made the laws, and that they would not dare to attempt an enforcement of any law of the land which was obnoxious to him."[202]

Another rare public revelation of infanticide was the 2014 case of a novice nun-in-training Sosefina Amoa. She was sentenced to four years in prison for smothering to death her newborn child at the Catholic Northeast Little Sisters of the Poor Convent in Washington, D.C. What made Amoa's case so unusual is that it was reported to the police at all. Judy Byington of Child Abuse Recovery stated that according to child abuse survivors of Catholic institutions, it is common for priests and nuns to kill newborn children and for the other nuns and priests to keep it quiet in order to protect the reputation of the Catholic Church.[203]

Infanticide seems to follow in the wake of Catholic priests. Irene Favel was a resident in a Canadian aboriginal school run by the Catholic Church. She reveals one chilling episode of a newborn baby being immolated alive in a furnace.

> I'm Irene Favel. I'm seventy five. I went to residential school in Muscowequan from 1944 to 1949, and I had a rough life. I was mistreated in every way. There was a young girl, and she was pregnant from a priest there. And what they did, she had her baby, and they took the baby, and wrapped it up in a nice pink outfit, and they took it downstairs where I was cooking dinner with the nun. And they took the baby into the furnace room, and they threw that little baby in there and burned it alive. All you could hear was this little cry, like "Uuh!", and that was it. You could smell that flesh cooking.[204]

That was not an isolated incident. Other former aboriginal Canadian students have told of similar immolations of newborn infants and aborted fetuses by Catholic nuns and priests at Canadian aboriginal schools.[205]

William H. Kennedy in his 2004 book, *Lucifer's Lodge*, explained that the large scale sexual abuse of Catholic nuns by priests and nuns continues unchecked today.

> According to the 1996 survey of nuns in the United States (which was intentionally never published by the [Roman Catholic] Church but was leaked by some Vatican insider), it is reported that a minimum of 34,000 Catholic nuns (about 40% of all American nuns) claim to have been sexually abused. Three of every four of these nuns claimed they were sexually victimized by a priest, nun, or other religious person. Two out of five nuns who stated they were sexually abused claimed that their exploitation included some form of genital contact. All nuns who claimed repeated sexual exploitation reported that they were pressured by religious superiors for sexual favors.[206]

The above survey cited by Kennedy included all nuns in both open and cloistered orders. The sexual abuse in cloistered nunneries is much more prevalent, as those nuns are virtual prisoners in their convents.

There have been several recent reports written by

senior members of women's religious orders that have documented the worldwide practice of priestly rape and sexual abuse of nuns.[207] The Vatican is unrepentant and has falsely characterized the sexual abuse of nuns by priests as being rare, isolated incidents.[208]

The European Parliament is not willing to go along with the Vatican denials. In 2001, the European Parliament approved an unprecedented motion that blamed the Vatican for rampant rapes suffered by nuns at the hands of Catholic priests in Africa.[209]

A Roman Catholic internet news agency, Zenit, reported:

> The parliamentary motion, on the "Responsibility of the Vatican in Regard to the Violation of Human Rights by Catholic Priests," has no executive character but rather is intended as a "moral judgment."
>
> It "condemns all the sexual violations against women, particularly against Catholic nuns. Likewise, it requests that the perpetrators of the crimes be arrested and handed over to justice."[210]

Margaret Shepherd (formerly a nun, Sister Magdalene Adelaide) describes the typical scene of the first experience of a young innocent cloistered nun being ravished by a priest of Rome.

> We leave the church, and, ascending twelve steps, find ourselves in a room comfortably

furnished. A man in the guise of a priest of Rome is seated on a sofa. The door opens, and the young girl we noticed in the church enters the room, and, as with down-cast eyes she kneels to receive the priest's blessing, a look of loathing and fear pastes over her features. "Come and sit down here, my daughter; I desire to speak with you." With trembling steps the girl approaches the sofa, and the priest, taking her hand, says: " Why so fearful of me, my child?" And, drawing her down beside him, he places his arm around her waist; his hot, liquor-fumed breath fans her cheek. His coarse sensual lips are pressed to hers; she shrinks away in loathing; her womanly modesty is outraged; she struggles to liberate herself— too late! Poor, helpless girl, she has not sufficient physical strength to overcome the wretch that holds her; her piercing cries for help are not heard outside the room. Exhausted, she lies in the grasp of this spiritual father, and before she leaves the room her purity has been violated, and she becomes the toy and convenience of this "protector" (sic) of morality.[211]

Charlotte Wells (her real surname was Keckler[212]) spent 22 years (from approximately 1910 until 1932) in a cloistered nunnery, before she finally escaped to tell her story to the world. She explained how the nuns in the cloistered nunnery were helpless objects of sexual pleasure for the priests. When the nuns inevitably became pregnant, their babies were murdered shortly after birth, and the bodies of the babies were disposed of in lime pits.

Here we are, a body of those little nuns. On this particular morning, the mother superior might say this, "We're all going to be lined up here." And I don't know what she's lining me up for. And then, you know, there might be ten others, there might be 15 others, and then she'll tell us all to strip and we have to take every stitch of our clothing off. ... And here we are, lined up, and here comes two or three Roman Catholic priests with liquor under their belts, and there they're going to march in front of those nude girls and choose the girl they want to take to the cell with them. These are convents, cloistered convents, not open orders. The priest can do anything he wants to and hide behind the cloak of religion. Then that same Roman Catholic priest will go back into the Roman Catholic churches and there he'll say Mass, and there he'll go into the confessional box and make those poor people believe he can give them absolution from their sins when he's full of sin. When he's full of corruption and vice, still he acts as their God. What a terrible thing it is. And on it goes. ... Then sometimes the priests come and they get angry at us because we refuse to sin with them voluntarily. And you know, after all, the nuns' bodies are broken after we're there awhile. And many, many the time, to have him strike you in the mouth is a terrible thing. I've had my front teeth knocked out. I know what it's all about. And then they get you down on the floor and then kick you in the stomach. Many of those precious little girls have babies under their heart, and it doesn't bother a priest to kick you in the stomach with a baby under your heart. He doesn't mind. The baby is going to be killed anyway because those babies are going to be born in the convent. ... They'll never bathe that baby's body, but he can only live four or five hours. And then the mother superior will take that baby and put her fingers in its nostrils, cover its mouth and snuff its little life out. ... And why do they build these lime pits in the convent? What is the reason for building them if it isn't to kill the babies? And that baby will be taken into the lime pit and chemical lime will be put over its body. And that's the end of babies.[213]

Charlotte Wells' testimony is belated corroboration of Maria Monk. The Catholic priests are the "natural brute beasts," to which God referred in 2 Peter 2:12. They are "made to be taken and destroyed," in hell by God, as they have "eyes full of adultery, and that cannot cease from sin; beguiling unstable souls: an heart they have exercised with covetous practices; cursed children: Which have forsaken the right way, and are gone astray. ... These are wells without water, clouds that are carried with a tempest; to whom the mist of darkness is reserved for ever. For when they speak great swelling words of vanity, they allure

through the lusts of the flesh, through much wantonness."
2 Peter 2:14-15,17-18.

Endnotes

1. Maria Monk, Awful Disclosures of the Hotel Dieu Nunnery of Montreal, 1836, http://www.reformation.org/maria-monk.html.

2. J. Bernard Delany, O.P., The Real Maria Monk, The Evangelization Station, http://www.evangelizationstation.com/htm_html/Anti-Catholicism/real_maria_monk.htm (last visited on December 28, 2014).

3. Maria Monk, Awful Disclosures of the Hotel Dieu Nunnery of Montreal, 1836, http://www.reformation.org/maria-monk.html.

4. Maria Monk, Awful Disclosures of the Hotel Dieu Nunnery of Montreal, 1836, http://www.reformation.org/maria-monk.html.

5. Maria Monk, Further Disclosures, at 89 (1837), addendum to J.J. Slocum, Confirmation of Maria Monk's Disclosures Concerning the Hotel Dieu Nunnery, http://ssoc.selfip.com:81/texts/1839__slocum__confirmation_of_maria_monks_disclosures.pdf.

6. Rosamond Culbertson, A Narrative of the Captivity and Sufferings of an American Female Under the Popish Priests, in the Island of Cuba; With a Full Disclosure of Their Manners and Customs, at 72 (1837).

7. Maria Monk, Account of The Attempts to Abduct Maria Monk (1837), at 4, addendum to J.J. Slocum, Confirmation of Maria Monk's Disclosures Concerning the Hotel Dieu Nunnery, http://ssoc.selfip.com:81/texts/1839_slocum_ _confirmation_of_maria_monks_disclosures.pd f.

8. Maria Monk, Account of The Attempts to Abduct Maria Monk (1837), addendum to J.J. Slocum, Confirmation of Maria Monk's Disclosures Concerning the Hotel Dieu Nunnery, http://ssoc.selfip.com:81/texts/1839_slocum_ _confirmation_of_maria_monks_disclosures.pd f.

9. Thurston, Herbert. "Impostors." The Catholic Encyclopedia. Vol. 7. New York: Robert Appleton Company, 1910. 24 Dec. 2014 <http://www.newadvent.org/cathen/07698b.htm>.

10. Maria Monk, Wikipedia, http://en.wikipedia.org/wiki/Maria_Monk#cite_note-3 (last visited on May 31, 2014).

11. Awful Exposure of the Atrocious Plot, at 126-129 (1836).

12. Maria Monk, Account of Attempt to Abduct Maria Monk, 1837, at 18, addendum to J.J. Slocum, Confirmation of Maria Monk's Disclosures Concerning the Hotel Dieu

Nunnery, http://ssoc.selfip.com:81/texts/1839__slocum__ _confirmation_of_maria_monks_disclosures.pdf.

13. Maria Monk, Account of Attempt to Abduct Maria Monk, 1837, at 18, addendum to J.J. Slocum, Confirmation of Maria Monk's Disclosures Concerning the Hotel Dieu Nunnery, http://ssoc.selfip.com:81/texts/1839__slocum__ _confirmation_of_maria_monks_disclosures.pdf.

14. Awful Exposure of the Atrocious Plot (1836).

15. Thomas E. Watson, Maria Monk and Her Revelations of Convent Crimes, 2nd Edition, p. 28 (1927), https://archive.org/stream/mariamonkherreve00wats#page/28/mode/2up.

16. Thomas E. Watson, Maria Monk and Her Revelations of Convent Crimes, 2nd Edition, p. 28 (1927), https://archive.org/stream/mariamonkherreve00wats#page/28/mode/2up.

17. Affidavit of Maria Monk's Mother, October 24, 1835, https://archive.org/stream/cihm_46628#page/n5/mode/2up.

18. Affidavit of Maria Monk's Mother, October 24, 1835, https://archive.org/stream/cihm_46628#page/n5/mode/2up.

19. J.J. Slocum, Confirmation of Maria Monk's Disclosures Concerning the Hotel Dieu Nunnery, 30-32, (1837) http://ssoc.selfip.com:81/texts/1839__slocum__confirmation_of_maria_monks_disclosures.pdf.

20. Barbara Ubryk, The Convent Horror, The Story of of Barbara Ubryk, Twenty-One Years in a Convent Dungeon Eight Feet Long, Six Feet Wide, from Official Records, Excerpted from the enlarged 1957 Edition, http://www.jesus-is-lord.com/barbara.htm.

21. Ford Hendrickson, The Black Convent Slave, at 77-115 (1914), https://archive.org/details/blackconventsla00hendgoog.

22. Ford Hendrickson, The Black Convent Slave, at 77-115 (1914), https://archive.org/details/blackconventsla00hendgoog.

23. Maria Monk, Awful Disclosures (with supplemental appendix), at 155-157 (1836).

24. Maria Monk, Maria Monk, Awful Disclosures (with supplemental appendix), at 344 (1836).

25. Evidence Demonstrating the Falsehoods of William Stone Concerning the Hotel Dieu Nunnery of Montreal, at 18 (1837), https://archive.org/details/cihm_57287.

26. *Falsehoods of William L. Stone*, at 15, https://archive.org/details/cihm_57287.

27. *Falsehoods of William L. Stone*, at 20, https://archive.org/details/cihm_57287.

28. William L. Stone, Maria Monk and the Nunnery of the Hotel Dieu, Being an Account of a Visit to the Convents of Montreal and Refutation of the "Awful Disclosures," 1836, at 8-9, https://archive.org/details/cihm_37485.

29. William L. Stone, Maria Monk and the Nunnery of the Hotel Dieu, Being an Account of a Visit to the Convents of Montreal and Refutation of the "Awful Disclosures," 1836, at 9, https://archive.org/details/cihm_37485

30. William L. Stone, Maria Monk and the Nunnery of the Hotel Dieu, Being an Account of a Visit to the Convents of Montreal and Refutation of the "Awful Disclosures," 1836, at 11, https://archive.org/details/cihm_37485

31. *Falsehoods of William L. Stone*, at 18.

32. *Falsehoods of William L. Stone*, at 4.

33. *Falsehoods of William L. Stone*, at 19.

34. Evidence Demonstrating the Falsehoods of William Stone Concerning the Hotel Dieu Nunnery of Montreal, at 18-19 (1837), https://archive.org/details/cihm_57287.

35. J.J. Slocum, Confirmation of Maria Monk's Disclosures Concerning the Hotel Dieu Nunnery, 1837, at 82.

36. Stone, Refutation of the "Awful Disclosures," at 28.

37. *Falsehoods of William L. Stone*, at 12.

38. Maria Monk, Awful Disclosures (with supplemental appendix), at 53 (1836).

39. Maria Monk, Further Disclosures, at 134-135 (1837), addendum to J.J. Slocum, Confirmation of Maria Monk's Disclosures Concerning the Hotel Dieu Nunnery, http://ssoc.selfip.com:81/texts/1839__slocum__ _confirmation_of_maria_monks_disclosures.pdf.

40. Ford Hendrickson, The Black Convent Slave, at 23 (1914), https://archive.org/details/blackconventsla00hendgoog.

41. Maria Monk, Awful Disclosures (with supplemental appendix), at 108-109 (1836).

42. Stone, Refutation of the "Awful Disclosures," at 31.

43. Stone, Refutation of the "Awful Disclosures," at 32.

44. *Falsehoods of William L. Stone*, at 5-6.

45. *Falsehoods of William L. Stone*, at 7.

46. *Falsehoods of William L. Stone*, at 8.

47. *Falsehoods of William L. Stone*, at 8.

48. Evidence Demonstrating the Falsehoods of William Stone Concerning the Hotel Dieu Nunnery of Montreal, at 9-10 (1837), https://archive.org/details/cihm_57287.

49. Stone, Refutation of the "Awful Disclosures," at 18.

50. *Falsehoods of William L. Stone*, at 4.

51. Maria Monk, Maria Monk, Awful Disclosures (with supplemental appendix), at 18 (1836) (French language recitation deleted).

52. Paul Serup, Who Killed Abraham Lincoln?, at 228 (2008).

53. Paul Serup, Who Killed Abraham Lincoln?, at 228-29 (2008), quoting The Life and Labours Of the Reverend Father Chiniquy, at 5 (1861).

54. LES GARETT, WHICH BIBLE CAN WE TRUST?, p. 16 (1982); *See also,* COLLIER'S ENCYCLOPEDIA, volume 22, p. 563.

55. Rebecca Theresa Reed, Six Months in a Convent, at 133 (1835).

56. Josephine M. Bunkley, *Miss Bunkley's Book*, The Testimony of an Escaped Novice from the Sisterhood of St. Joseph, Emettsburg, Maryland, The Mother-House of the Sisters of Charity in the United States, at 225 (1855). Please note that there is apparently an extant unauthorized version of Miss Bunkley's book that was published without Miss Bunkley's permission. Miss Bunkley warned that while the book was based upon part of her original manuscript, it was revised without her permission. Miss Bunkley successfully sued to prevent its publication of that book in the U.S. The unauthorized version ended up being published in England by Allman and Son and is titled in pertinent part "The Escaped Nun." Miss Bunkley's authorized version was published in the U.S. by Harper and Brothers and is titled in pertinent part "The Testimony of an Escaped Novice."

57. Samuel B. Smith, Decisive Confirmation of the Awful Disclosures of Maria Monk, 1836, https://archive.org/details/cihm_60942.

58. Patrick Phelan, Dictionary of Canadien Biography, http://www.biographi.ca/en/bio.php?id_nbr=4133 (last visited on May 10, 2014).

59.Maria Monk, Maria Monk, Awful Disclosures (with supplemental appendix), at 45-46 (1836).

60.Maria Monk, Awful Disclosures (with supplemental appendix), at 97-104 (1836).

61.Fed. R. Evid. 804.

62.Maria Monk, Maria Monk, Awful Disclosures (with supplemental appendix), at 345 (1836).

63.Maria Monk, Maria Monk, Awful Disclosures (with supplemental appendix), at 338 (1836).

64.Maria Monk, Maria Monk, Awful Disclosures (with supplemental appendix), at 312 (1836).

65.Patrick Phelan, Dictionary of Canadien Biography, http://www.biographi.ca/en/bio.php?id_nbr=4133 (last visited on May 10, 2014).

66.Maria Monk, Maria Monk, Awful Disclosures (with supplemental appendix), at 346 (1836).

67.Samuel B. Smith, Decisive Confirmation of the Awful Disclosures of Maria Monk, 1836, https://archive.org/details/cihm_60942.

68. Maria Monk, Awful Disclosures of the Hotel Dieu Nunnery of Montreal, With Appendix and Supplement Giving Particulars of the Nunnery and Grounds, Second Edition Revised by J. J. Slocum, at 331-32 (1837), https://archive.org/details/awfuldisclosure00monkgoog.

69. *Evidence Demonstrating the Falsehoods of William L. Stone Concerning the Hotel Dieu Nunnery of Montreal*, 1837, at 24-25, https://archive.org/details/cihm_57287.

70. *Evidence Demonstrating the Falsehoods of William L. Stone Concerning the Hotel Dieu Nunnery of Montreal*, 1837, at 24-25, https://archive.org/details/cihm_57287.

71. *Falsehoods of William L. Stone*, at 19.

72. Maria Monk, Account of Attempt to Abduct Maria Monk, 1837, at 18, addendum to J.J. Slocum, Confirmation of Maria Monk's Disclosures Concerning the Hotel Dieu Nunnery, http://ssoc.selfip.com:81/texts/1839__slocum__ _confirmation_of_maria_monks_disclosures.pdf.

73. Maria Monk, Maria Monk, Awful Disclosures (with supplemental appendix), at 367 (1836).

74. Maria Monk, Maria Monk, Awful Disclosures (with supplemental appendix), at

367 (1836).

75. Maria Monk, Maria Monk, Awful Disclosures (with supplemental appendix), at 367 (1836).

76. Thurston, Herbert. "Impostors." The Catholic Encyclopedia. Vol. 7. New York: Robert Appleton Company, 1910. 17 May 2014 <http://www.newadvent.org/cathen/07698b.htm>.

77. J.J. Slocum, Confirmation of Maria Monk's Disclosures Concerning the Hotel Dieu Nunnery, 1837, at 28, http://ssoc.selfip.com:81/texts/1839__slocum__ _confirmation_of_maria_monks_disclosures.pdf.

78. J.J. Slocum, Confirmation of Maria Monk's Disclosures Concerning the Hotel Dieu Nunnery, 1837, at 28.

79. J.J. Slocum, Confirmation of Maria Monk's Disclosures Concerning the Hotel Dieu Nunnery, 1837, at 42.

80. J.J. Slocum, Confirmation of Maria Monk's Disclosures Concerning the Hotel Dieu Nunnery, 1837, at 42.

81. J.J. Slocum, Confirmation of Maria Monk's Disclosures Concerning the Hotel Dieu Nunnery, 1837, at 42.

82. J.J. Slocum, Confirmation of Maria Monk's Disclosures Concerning the Hotel Dieu Nunnery, 1837, at 43.

83. J.J. Slocum, Confirmation of Maria Monk's Disclosures Concerning the Hotel Dieu Nunnery, 1837, at 44-45.

84. J.J. Slocum, Confirmation of Maria Monk's Disclosures Concerning the Hotel Dieu Nunnery, 1837, at 45-46.

85. EDMOND PARIS, THE SECRET HISTORY OF THE JESUITS, p. 64 (1975).

86. Jesuitical, Oxford Dictionary, http://www.oxforddictionaries.com/definition/english/Jesuitical (last visited on May 8, 2014).

87. Jesuitical, Noah Webster, American Dictionary of the English Language, 1828, http://webstersdictionary1828.com/.

88. John Spano, Catholic Doctrine Is Cited in Priest Sex Abuse Cases, Los Angeles Times, March 26, 2007, http://articles.latimes.com/2007/mar/26/local/me-priest26.

89. John Spano, Catholic Doctrine Is Cited in Priest Sex Abuse Cases, Los Angeles Times, March 26, 2007, http://articles.latimes.com/2007/mar/26/local/me-priest26.

90. John Spano, Catholic Doctrine Is Cited in Priest Sex Abuse Cases, Los Angeles Times, March 26, 2007, http://articles.latimes.com/2007/mar/26/local/me-priest26.

91. John Spano, Catholic Doctrine Is Cited in Priest Sex Abuse Cases, Los Angeles Times, March 26, 2007, http://articles.latimes.com/2007/mar/26/local/me-priest26.

92. Would a Priest or Bishop Lie under Oath? Mental Reservation Debated in Court Wednesday Re Church Witnesses Refusing to Answer in Depositions, City of Angels, May 17, 2007, http://www.bishop-accountability.org/news2007/05_06/2007_05_17_CityOfAngels_.htm.

93. Sister Charlotte (as told to Sister Nilah), From Convent to Pentecost, My Escape From the Cloistered Convent, 1999. See also, The Sister Charlotte Keckler Story, The Horrors Deep Within The Church Of Rome, http://jesus-messiah.com/charlotte/html/charlotte.html (last visited on April 15, 2014).

94. David A. Plaisted, Estimates of the Number Killed by the Papacy in the Middle Ages and Later, 2006, http://predoc.org/docs/index-10153.html?page=9. Also available online in HTML at http://www.cs.unc.edu/~plaisted/estimates.html

.

95. Alberto Rivera, ALBERTO, at 12 (1979).

96. Julia McNair Wright, Secrets of the Convent and Confessional, footnote at 254-255 (1876).

97. Julia McNair Wright, Secrets of the Convent and Confessional, footnote at 254 (1876).

98. Confirmation of Maria Monk's Disclosures, at 165 (1837), quoting, Hulderic Epist. adv. constit, de Cleric. Celib.

99. Sam Jordison, Magedine Laundries, February 5, 2014, http://samdjordison.blogspot.com/2013/02/magdalene-laundries.html.

100. William L. Stone, Maria Monk and the Nunnery of the Hotel Dieu, Being an Account of a Visit to the Convents of Montreal and Refutation of the "Awful Disclosures," 1836, at 31, https://archive.org/details/cihm_37485

101. The Sister Charlotte Keckler Story, November 28, 2011, http://wesdancin.wordpress.com/2011/11/28/the-sister-charlotte-keckler-story-the-horrors-deep-within-the-church-of-rome-get-this-to-every-female-male-woman-man-of-all-ages-all-parents-all-grand-parents-2/.

102. Josephine M. Bunkley, *Miss Bunkley's Book*, The Testimony of an Escaped Novice

from the Sisterhood of St. Joseph, Emettsburg, Maryland, The Mother-House of the Sisters of Charity in the United States, at 91 and 216 (1855).

103.Bunkley, at 252.

104.Bunkley, at 256-58.

105.Bunkley, at 255.

106.Lewis Hippolytus and Joseph Tonna, Nuns and Nunneries: Sketches Compiled Entirely from Romish Authorities, at 62 (1852).

107.Hippolytus and Tonna, at 62.

108.Hippolytus and Tonna, at 63.

109.
Hippolytus and Tonna, at 63.

110.The Escaped Nun: or, Disclosures of Convent Life; and Confessions of a Sister of Charity, at 96-97 (1855).

111.The Escaped Nun, at 98-99.

112.The Escaped Nun, at 104.

113.The Escaped Nun, at 104.

114.The Escaped Nun, at 105.

115.The Escaped Nun, at 106.

116.Personal Sacrifices for Faith, ABC 20/20, May 11, 2007, https://www.youtube.com/watch?v=Tm_8MUct7VA.

117.Personal Sacrifices for Faith, ABC 20/20, May 11, 2007, https://www.youtube.com/watch?v=Tm_8MUct7VA.

118.Personal Sacrifices for Faith, ABC 20/20, May 11, 2007, https://www.youtube.com/watch?v=Tm_8MUct7VA.

119.Josephine M. Bunkley, *Miss Bunkley's Book*, The Testimony of an Escaped Novice from the Sisterhood of St. Joseph, Emettsburg, Maryland, The Mother-House of the Sisters of Charity in the United States, at 282(1855).

120.Josephine M. Bunkley, *Miss Bunkley's Book*, The Testimony of an Escaped Novice from the Sisterhood of St. Joseph, Emettsburg, Maryland, The Mother-House of the Sisters of Charity in the United States, at 282(1855).

121.Bunkley at 286-87.

122.Bunkley at 291-92.

123.*Draper v. United States*, 358 U.S. 307 (1959); *See Illinois v. Gates*, 462 U.S. 213, 103 S. Ct. 2317 (1983); *See also Hill v. California*, 401 U.S. 797, 91 S. Ct. 1106 (1971) and *Carroll v. United States*, 267 U.S. 131,162 (1924).

124. *Adams v. Williams*, 407 U.S. 143, 145-46 (1972); *Terry v. Ohio*, 392 U.S. 1, 21-23 (1968); *United States v. Cortez*, 449 U.S. 411, 417 (1981).

125. False Imprisonment, http://injury.findlaw.com/torts-and-personal-injuries/false-imprisonment.html (last visited on February 4, 2015).

126. The Escaped Nun, or Disclosures of Convent Life, and the Confessions of a Sister of Charity, 340-43 (1855). The authorship of this book has been erroneously attributed to Josephine Bunkley. After having carefully read the book and compared it to the historical facts of Miss Bunkley's life, it is clear to this writer that it was not written by Miss Bunkley. It has all of the earmarks of a genuine account of an escaped nun who wished to remain anonymous and for that reason did not put her name to the book as the author.

127. David A. Plaisted, Estimates of the Number Killed by the Papacy in the Middle Ages and Later, at 70-71 (2006).

128. Claude R. Louks, June 10, 1885 - November 10, 1947, http://www.findagrave.com/cgi-bin/fg.cgi?page=gr&GRid=46323097.

129. Claude R. Louks, June 10, 1885 - November 10, 1947, http://www.findagrave.com/cgi-bin/fg.cgi?page=gr&GRid=46323097.

130. Tipton Tribune, July 7, 1931, http://www.newspapers.com/newspage/3341918 5/.

131. Claude R. Louks, June 10, 1885 - November 10, 1947, http://www.findagrave.com/cgi-bin/fg.cgi?page=gr&GRid=46323097.

132. Congregation of Saint Joseph Convent, http://www.csjoseph.org/tipton_indiana.aspx (last visited on March 7, 2015).

133. Bunkley at 299-302, citing Papism in the United States, by Robert J. Breckinridge, D.D., p. 235-245.

134. Bunkley at 302-303.

135. Sister Jesme, Amen, The Autobiography of a Nun, location 920 of 2274 in Kindle reader. (2009).

136. Sister Jesme, location 920 of 2274 in Kindle reader.

137. Bunkley at 305.

138. Bunkley at 305-22.

139. Stone, Refutation of the "Awful Disclosures," at 25.

140. Maria Monk, Maria Monk, Awful Disclosures (with supplemental appendix), at 160 (1836) (French language recitation deleted).

141. Maria Monk, Maria Monk, Awful Disclosures (with supplemental appendix), at 351-52 (1836) (French language recitation deleted).

142. Maria Monk, Further Disclosures, at 144, et. seq.(1837), addendum to J.J. Slocum, Confirmation of Maria Monk's Disclosures Concerning the Hotel Dieu Nunnery, http://ssoc.selfip.com:81/texts/1839__slocum__ _confirmation_of_maria_monks_disclosures.pdf

143. Maria Monk, Awful Disclosures (with supplemental appendix), at 148 (1836).

144. J.J. Slocum, Confirmation of Maria Monk's Disclosures Concerning the Hotel Dieu Nunnery, at 121 (1837).

145. J.J. Slocum, Confirmation of Maria Monk's Disclosures Concerning the Hotel Dieu Nunnery, at 121 (1837).

146. Samuel B. Smith, The Escape of Sainte Frances Patrick, Another Nun from the Hotel Dieu Nunnery, to Which is Appended a

Decisive Confirmation of the Awful Disclosures of Maria Monk (1836).

147. Maria Monk, Awful Disclosures of Maria Monk; or, The Hidden Secrets of a Nun's Life in a Convent Exposed, at 18 (1836), https://archive.org/details/cihm_38362.

148. Awful Exposure of the Atrocious Plot Formed by Certain Individuals Against the Clergy and Nuns of Lower Canada Through the Intervention of Maria Monk, at 36, (1836), https://archive.org/details/cihm_27925 (last visited on January 15, 2015).

149. Samuel B. Smith, The Escape of Sainte Frances Patrick, Another Nun from the Hotel Dieu Nunnery, to Which is Appended a Decisive Confirmation of the Awful Disclosures of Maria Monk (1836).

150. Mackey's Encyclopedia of Freemasonry, http://www.masonicdictionary.com/oath.html (last visited on April 17, 2014).

151. William L. Stone, Letters on Freemasonry and Anti-Freemasonry Addressed to the Honorable John Quincy Adams, 1832, at 66.

152. William L. Stone, Letters on Freemasonry and Anti-Freemasonry Addressed to the Honorable John Quincy Adams, 1832, at 67.

153. William L. Stone, Letters on Freemasonry and Anti-Freemasonry Addressed to the

Honorable John Quincy Adams, 1832, at 68.

154. JIM SHAW (33rd Degree Mason, Knight Commander of the Court of Honor, Past Worshipful Master of the Blue Lodge, Past Master of All Scottish Rite Bodies) and TOM MCKENNEY, THE DEADLY DECEPTION, Freemasonry Exposed by One of Its Top Leaders, p. 137 (1988).

155. DES GRIFFIN, THE FOURTH REICH OF THE RICH, p. 70 (1993).

156. Martin L. Wagner, Freemasonry: An Interpretation, at 85-86 (1912), available at http://www.mindserpent.com/American_History/organization/mason/freemasonry/freemasonry.html.

157. Wagner, at 338.

158. Stephen Knight, The Brotherhood, at 236 (1986).

159. Wagner, at 338.

160. Knight, at 236.

161. Wagner, at 338.

162. Knight, at 236.

163. DES GRIFFIN, THE FOURTH REICH OF THE RICH, p. 70 (1993).

164. ERIC JON PHELPS, VATICAN ASSASSINS: "WOUNDED IN THE HOUSE OF MY FRIENDS," p. 180 (2001).

165. NESTA WEBSTER, SECRET SOCIETIES AND SUBVERSIVE MOVEMENTS, http://web.archive.org/web/20021005055527/http://www.plausiblefutures.com/text/SS.html (website address current as of 2-28-05) (footnotes contained in original text omitted).

166. JIM SHAW (33rd Degree Mason, Knight Commander of the Court of Honor, Past Worshipful Master of the Blue Lodge, Past Master of All Scottish Rite Bodies) and TOM MCKENNEY, THE DEADLY DECEPTION, Freemasonry Exposed by One of Its Top Leaders, p. 137 (1988).

167. Barbara Aho, *Mystery, Babylon the Great - Catholic or Jewish?*, Watch Unto Prayer, *at* http://watch.pair.com/mystery-babylon.html (last visited on February 8, 2010) (citing "The Pope of the Council, Part 19: John XXIII and Masonry," Sodalitium, October/November 1996).

168. The Scandals and Heresies of John XXIII, http://www.mostholyfamilymonastery.com/13JohnXXIII.pdf, citing Paul I. Murphy and R. Rene Arlington, La Popessa, 1983, pp. 332-333.

169. The Scandals and Heresies of John XXIII, http://www.mostholyfamilymonastery.com/13_JohnXXIII.pdf, quoting Giovanni Cubeddu, 30 Days, Issue No. 2-1994., p. 25. See also, Mary Ball Martinez, The Undermining of the Catholic Church, Hillmac, Mexico, 1999, p. 117.

170. Alberto Rivera, Alberto, Part One, at 27.

171. *Evidence Demonstrating the Falsehoods of William L. Stone Concerning the Hotel Dieu Nunnery of Montreal*, 1837, at 2, https://archive.org/details/cihm_57287.

172. *Evidence Demonstrating the Falsehoods of William L. Stone Concerning the Hotel Dieu Nunnery of Montreal*, 1837, at 3, https://archive.org/details/cihm_57287.

173. *Evidence Demonstrating the Falsehoods of William L. Stone Concerning the Hotel Dieu Nunnery of Montreal*, 1837, at 3, https://archive.org/details/cihm_57287.

174. Thomas E. Watson, Maria Monk and Her Revelations of Convent Crimes, 2nd Edition, p. 23 (1927).

175. Thomas E. Watson, Maria Monk and Her Revelations of Convent Crimes, 2nd Edition, pp. 23-26 (1927).

176. Watson at 26.

177. Watson at 30.

178. Watson at 30.

179. Watson at 33.

180. Watson at 33-34.

181. Sarah J. Richardson, Life in the Grey Nunnery at Montreal, 212 (1858).

182. Sarah J. Richardson, Life in the Grey Nunnery at Montreal, 209 (1858).

183. Sarah J. Richardson, Life in the Grey Nunnery at Montreal, 134-139 (1858).

184. Darryl Eberhart, Sexual Abuse in the Roman Catholic Church, October 16, 2009, http://www.toughissues.org/handoutsnew/Sexual%20Abuse.htm, quoting Peter de Rosa, Vicars of Christ, at 404 and 408 (1988).

185. Sister Jesme, Amen, The Autobiography of a Nun (2009).

186. Sex, Violence, Corruption, Insider Exposes Rock the Kerala Church, Arjunpuri in Qatar, 17 July 2012, http://arjunpuriinqatar.blogspot.com/2012/07/sex-violence-corruption-insider-exposes.html.

187. Kerala Church Hit by Another Former Nun's Tell-all Book, Hindustan Times, Thiruvananthapuram, April 29, 2012,

http://www.hindustantimes.com/india-news/kerala-church-hit-by-another-former-nun-s-tell-all-book/article1-848193.aspx.

188. Kannur, Former Nun's Book Criticises Church Hypocrisy, WebIndia123, April 29, 2012, http://news.webindia123.com/news/articles/India/20120429/1974419.html.

189. George Kommattathil, Kannur, India, "Abortions Are Commonplace in Convents," - Sister Mary Chandy, Kerala Catholic Community, April 10, 2012, http://joyvarocky.blogspot.com/2012/05/abortions-are-commonplace-in-convents.html.

190. George Kommattathil, Kannur, India, Former 'Nun' Claims Abuse Rife, UCANEWS.com, April 10, 2012, http://www.ucanews.com/news/former-nun-claims-abuse-rife-in-convents/46938.

191. Sex, Violence, Corruption, Insider Exposes Rock the Kerala Church, Arjunpuri in Qatar, 17 July 2012, http://arjunpuriinqatar.blogspot.com/2012/07/sex-violence-corruption-insider-exposes.html.

192. Jose Kurien, Writer Regrets Helping 'Nun' Mary Chandy, Kerala Catholic Community, July 31, 2012, http://joyvarocky.blogspot.com/2012/08/nun-mary-chandy.html.

193. Kerala Sister's Book Runs Into Controversy, 12 August 2012, http://twocircles.net/2012aug12/kerala_sisters_book_runs_controversy.html.

194. Kerala Sister's Book Runs Into Controversy, supra.

195. E.g., Fed. R. Evid. 803 (7).

196. Judy Byington, Child Abuse Recovery, March 19, 2014, http://childabuserecovery.com/are-catholic-priests-and-nuns-murdering-their-own-children/.

197. Judy Byington, Child Abuse Recovery, supra.

198. Schenectady Gazette, March 4, 1977, http://news.google.com/newspapers?nid=1917&dat=19770304&id=LTkwAAAAIBAJ&sjid=jeAFAAAAIBAJ&pg=2428,1155129.

199. Catholic Courier Journal, at 19, June 14, 1972, http://lib.catholiccourier.com/1972-courier-journal/courier-journal-1972%20-%200581.pdf.

200. Catholic Courier Journal, supra.

201. Catholic Courier Journal, supra.

202. The Escaped Nun, or Disclosures of Convent Life, and the Confessions of a Sister of Charity, 340-43 (1855). The authorship of

this book has been erroneously attributed to Josephine Bunkley. After having carefully read the book and compared it to the historical facts of Miss Bunkley's life, it is clear to this writer that it was not written by Miss Bunkley. It has all of the earmarks of a genuine account of an escaped nun who wished to remain anonymous and for that reason did not put her name to the book as the author.

203. Judy Byington, Child Abuse Recovery, March 19, 2014, http://childabuserecovery.com/are-catholic-priests-and-nuns-murdering-their-own-children/.

204. Witness to murder at Indian Residential School, November 16, 2008, https://www.youtube.com/watch?v=CReISnQDbBE. See also, Kevin D. Annett, The Canadian Holocaust: Hidden No Longer, January 24, 2012, http://wariscrime.com/new/the-canadian-holocaust-hidden-no-longer/.

205. Appeal from Survivors of Canadian Genocide, at 9:00-10:00, April 8, 2013, https://www.youtube.com/watch?v=cVYkctM1k90&feature=youtu.be.

206. Darryl Eberhart, Sexual Abuse in the Roman Catholic Church, October 16, 2009, http://www.toughissues.org/handoutsnew/Sexual%20Abuse.htm, quoting William H. Kennedy, Lucifer's Lodge: Satanic Ritual

Abuse in the Catholic Church, at 179 (2009), who in turn quoted the Boston Globe, January 1, 2002.

207. The Nuns' Stories, Vatican Condemned for Abuse of Nuns by Priests, http://archives.weirdload.com/nuns.html (Last visited on April 17, 2014).

208. The Nuns' Stories, Vatican Condemned for Abuse of Nuns by Priests, http://archives.weirdload.com/nuns.html (Last visited on April 17, 2014).

209. European Parliament Assails Vatican Over Abuse Cases, April 6, 2001, http://www.zenit.org/en/articles/european-parliament-assails-vatican-over-abuse-cases.

210. European Parliament Assails Vatican Over Abuse Cases, April 6, 2001, http://www.zenit.org/en/articles/european-parliament-assails-vatican-over-abuse-cases.

211. Margaret Shepherd, My Life in the Convent: or The Marvelous Personal Experiences of Margaret Shepherd, 206-207 (1892), https://archive.org/details/mylifeinconvento00shepuoft.

212. The Sister Charlotte Keckler Story, November 28, 2011, http://wesdancin.wordpress.com/2011/11/28/the-sister-charlotte-keckler-story-the-horrors-dee

p-within-the-church-of-rome-get-this-to-every-female-male-woman-man-of-all-ages-all-parents-all-grand-parents-2/.

213. The Testimony of Charlotte Wells, http://www.jesus-is-lord.com/charlot1.htm (last visited on May 12, 2014). See also, From Convent to Pentecost, My Escape From the Cloistered Convent, As told to Sister Nilah by Sister Charlotte (1999).

Other books available from Great Mountain Publishing:

9/11-Enemies Foreign and Domestic
ISBN-13: 978-0983262732

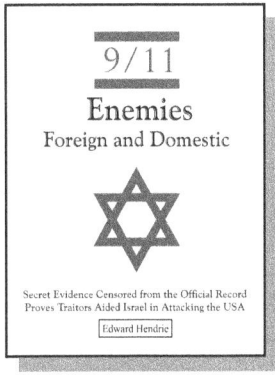

9/11-Enemies Foreign and Domestic proves beyond a reasonable doubt that the U.S. Government's conspiracy theory of the attacks on September 11, 2001, is a preposterous cover story. The evidence in 9/11-Enemies Foreign and Domestic has been suppressed from the official government reports and censored from the mass media. The evidence proves that powerful Zionists ordered the 9/11 attacks, which were perpetrated by Israel's Mossad, aided and abetted by treacherous high officials in the U.S. Government. 9/11-Enemies Foreign and Domestic identifies the traitors by name and details their subversive crimes. There is sufficient evidence in 9/11-Enemies Foreign and Domestic to indict important officials of the U.S. Government for high treason. The reader will understand how the U.S. Government really works and what Sir John Harrington (1561-1612) meant when he said: "Treason doth never prosper: what's the reason? Why if it prosper, none dare call it treason." There are millions of Americans who have taken an oath to defend the U.S. Constitution against all enemies foreign and domestic. The mass media, which is under the control of a disloyal cabal, keeps those patriotic Americans ignorant of the traitors among them. J. Edgar Hoover, former Director of the FBI, explained: "The individual is handicapped by coming face-to-face with a conspiracy so monstrous-he simply cannot believe it exists." 9/11-Enemies Foreign and Domestic erases any doubt about the existence of the monstrous conspiracy described by Hoover and arms the reader with the knowledge required to save our great nation. "My people are destroyed for lack of knowledge." Hosea 4:6.

Solving the Mystery of BABYLON THE GREAT
ISBN-13: 978-0983262701

"Attorney and Christian researcher Edward Hendrie investigates and reveals one of the greatest exposés of all time. . . . a book you don't want to miss. Solving the Mystery of Babylon the Great is packed with documentation. Never before have the crypto-Jews who seized the reins of power in Rome been put under such intense scrutiny." Texe Marrs, Power of Prophecy. The evidence presented in this book leads to the ineluctable conclusion that the Roman Catholic Church was established by crypto-Jews as a false "Christian" front for a Judaic/Babylonian religion. That religion is the core of a world conspiracy against man and God. That is not a conspiracy theory based upon speculation, but rather the hard truth based upon authoritative evidence, which is documented in this book. Texe Marrs explains in his foreword to the book: "Who is Mystery Babylon? What is the meaning of the sinister symbols found in these passages? Which city is being described as the 'great city' so full of sin and decadence, and who are its citizens? Why do the woman and beast of Revelation seek the destruction of the holy people, the saints and martyrs of Jesus? What does it all mean for you and me today? Solving the Mystery of Babylon the Great answers these questions and more. Edward Hendrie's discoveries are not based on prejudice but on solid evidence aligned forthrightly with the 'whole counsel of God.' He does not condone nor will he be a part of any project in which Bible verses are taken out of context, or in which scriptures are twisted to mean what they do not say. Again and again you will find that Mr. Hendrie documents his assertions, backing up what he says with historical facts and proofs. Most important is that he buttresses his findings with scriptural understanding. The foundation for his research is sturdy because it is based on the bedrock of God's unshakeable Word."

The Anti-Gospel
ISBN-13: 978-0983262749

Edward Hendrie uses God's word to strip the sheep's clothing from false Christian ministers and expose them as ravening wolves preaching an anti-gospel. The anti-gospel is based on a myth that all men have a will that is free from the bondage of sin to choose whether to believe in Jesus. The Holy Bible, however, states that all men are spiritually dead and cannot believe in Jesus unless they are born again of the Holy Spirit. Ephesians 2:1-7; John 3:3-8. God has chosen his elect to be saved by his grace through faith in Jesus Christ. Ephesians 1:3-9; 2:8-10. God imbues his elect with the faith needed to believe in Jesus. Hebrews 12:2; John 1:12-13. The devil's false gospel contradicts the word of

God and reverses the order of things. Under the anti-gospel, instead of a sovereign God choosing his elect, sovereign man decides whether to choose God. The calling of the Lord Jesus Christ is effectual; all who are chosen for salvation will believe in Jesus. John 6:37-44. The anti-gospel has a false Jesus, who only offers the possibility of salvation, with no assurance. The anti-gospel blasphemously makes God out to be a liar by denying the total depravity of man and the sovereign election of God. All who preach that false gospel are under a curse from God. Galatians 1:6-9.

Bloody Zion
ISBN-13: 978-0983262763

Jesus told Pontius Pilate: "My kingdom is not of this world." John 18:36. God has a spiritual Zion that is in a heavenly Jerusalem. Hebrews 12:22; Revelation 21:10. Jesus Christ is the chief corner stone laid by God in Zion. 1 Peter 2:6. Those who believe in Jesus Christ are living stones in the spiritual house of God. 1 Peter 2:5; Ephesians 2:20-22. Believers are in Jesus and Jesus is in believers. John 14:20; 17:20-23. All who are elected by God to believe in Jesus Christ are part of the heavenly Zion, without regard to whether they are Jews or Gentiles. Romans 10:12. Satan is a great adversary of God, who has created his own mystery religions. During the Babylonian captivity (2 Chronicles 36:20), an occult society of Jews replaced God's commands with Satan's Babylonian dogma. Their new religion became Judaism. Jesus explained the corruption of the Judaic religion: "Howbeit in vain do they worship me, teaching for doctrines the commandments of men." Mark 7:7. Jesus revealed the Satanic origin of Judaism when he stated: "Ye are of your father the devil, and the lusts of your father ye will do." John 8:44. Babylonian Judaism remains the religion of the Jews today. Satan has infected many nominal "Christian" denominations with his Babylonian occultism, which has given rise to "Christian" Zionism. "Christian" Zionism advocates a counterfeit, earthly Zion, within which fleshly Jews take primacy over the spiritual church of Jesus Christ. This book exposes "Christian" Zionism as a false gospel and subversive political movement that sustains Israel's war against God and man.

What Shall I Do to Inherit Eternal Life?
ISBN-13: 978-0983262770

A certain ruler posed to Jesus the most important question ever asked: "Good Master, what shall I do to inherit eternal life?" (Luke 18:18) The man came to the right person. Jesus is God, and therefore his answer to that question is authoritative. This book examines Jesus' surprising answer and definitively explains how one inherits eternal life. This is a book about God's revelation to man. Except for the Holy Bible, this is the most important book you will ever read.

Antichrist: The Beast Revealed
ISBN-13: 978-0-9832627-8-7

The antichrist is among us, here and now. This book proves it by comparing the biblical prophecies about the antichrist with the evidence that those prophecies have been fulfilled. This book documents the man of sin's esoteric confession that he is the antichrist. You will learn how the antichrist has changed times and laws as prophesied by Daniel, and how he is today sitting in the temple of God, "shewing himself that he is God," in fulfillment of Paul's prophecy in 2 Thessalonians 2:4. The beast of Revelation has come into the world, "after the working of Satan with all power and signs and lying wonders, and with all deceivableness of unrighteousness," as prophesied in 2 Thessalonians 2:10. The antichrist's adeptness as a hypocrite is the reason for his evil success. Indeed, to be the antichrist, his evil character must be concealed beneath a facade of piety. "And no marvel; for Satan himself is transformed into an angel of light. Therefore it is no great thing if his ministers also be transformed as the ministers of righteousness; whose end shall be according to their works." 2 Corinthians 11:14-15. The key to revealing the identity of the antichrist is to uncover his hypocrisy. Because the hypocrisy of the antichrist is so extreme, those who have been hoodwinked by his religious doctrines will be shocked to learn of it. This book exposes the concealed iniquity of the antichrist and juxtaposes it against his publicly proclaimed false persona of righteousness, thus bringing into clear relief that man of sin, the son of perdition, who is truly a ravening wolf in sheep's clothing, speaking lies in hypocrisy. See Matthew 7:15 and 1 Timothy 4:1-3.

Rome's Responsibility for the Assassination of Abraham Lincoln, With an Appendix Containing Conversations Between Abraham Lincoln and Charles Chiniquy
ISBN-13: 978-0983262794

The author of this book, General Thomas Maley Harris, was a medical doctor, who recruited and served as commander of the Tenth West Virginia Volunteers during the Civil War. He rose in rank through meritorious service to become a brigadier general in the Union Army. General Harris established a reputation for faithfulness, industriousness, intelligence, and efficiency. He was noted for his leadership in preparing his troops and leading them in battle. He was brevetted a major general for "gallant conduct in the assault on Petersburg." After the Civil War, General Harris served one term as a representative in the West Virginia legislature, and was West Virginia's Adjutant General from 1869 to 1870. General Harris was a member of the Military Commission that tried and convicted the conspirators who assassinated President Abraham Lincoln. He had first hand knowledge of the sworn testimony of the witnesses in that trial. This book summarizes the salient evidence brought out during the military trial and adds information from other sources to present before the public the ineluctable conclusion that the assassination of Abraham Lincoln was the work of the Roman Catholic Church. The Roman Catholic Church has been largely successful in suppressing the circulation of this book. This book has never been given a place on bookstore shelves, as it exposed too much for the Roman Catholic hierarchy to tolerate. Any display of this book would bring an instant boycott of the bookstore. It is only now, in the age of the internet, where the marketplace of ideas has been opened wide, that this book can be found by those searching for the truth of who was behind the assassination of Abraham Lincoln.

The above books can be ordered from bookstores and from internet sites, including, but not limited to: www.antichristconspiracy.com, www.lulu.com, www.911enemies.com, www.mysterybabylonthegreat.net, www.antigospel.com, https://play.google.com, www.barnesandnoble.com, and www.amazon.com.

Edward Hendrie
edwardhendrie@gmail.com

www.ingramcontent.com/pod-product-compliance
Lightning Source LLC
Chambersburg PA
CBHW051120160426
43195CB00014B/2281